D0361714

[CONFIDENTIAL]

FORBIDDEN KNOWLEDGE:

101 THINGS **NOT** EVERYONE SHOULD KNOW HOW TO DO

Michael Powell

Adams Media

New York   London   Toronto   Sydney   New Delhi

Aadams media

Adams Media
An Imprint of Simon & Schuster, Inc.
57 Littlefield Street
Avon, Massachusetts 02322
Copyright © 2007 by Gusto Company AS.

For information about special discounts for bulk purchases, please contact Simon & Schuster Special Sales at 1-866-506-1949 or business@simonandschuster.com.

The Simon & Schuster Speakers Bureau can bring authors to your live event. For more information or to book an event contact the Simon & Schuster Speakers Bureau at 1-866-248-3049 or visit our website at www.simonspeakers.com.

Interior design by Allen Boe

Illustrations by Allen Boe and © iStockphoto.com

Photographs © iStockphoto.com

Manufactured in China

20 19 18 17 16 15 14

Library of Congress Cataloging-in-Publication Data has been applied for.

ISBN 978-1-59869-525-0

[CONFIDENTIAL]

FORBIDDEN KNOWLEDGE:

101 THINGS **NOT** EVERYONE
SHOULD KNOW HOW TO DO

INTRODUCTION:

There are lots of books which tell you how to do stuff that you really should know how to do, like making the bed or tying a Windsor knot. But have you ever wondered about the things you really should NOT know how to do, like counterfeiting money, sawing a woman in half, or staging a military coup?

Now we're not suggesting that you go out and start being an antisocial menace, but that doesn't stop you from being curious about how it's done, right? This book has been written in the same spirit as one might teach tax law to a horse—the information will pique your curiosity, but we hope that you'll never have occasion to use it.

In fact, dipping into this dysfunctional directory might act as a preventative measure. For example, if you find yourself inadvertently jamming a screwdriver into the ignition of a Lincoln Continental (see page 55), awake from your criminal torpor and realize that you are committing a car-based felony. Worse still, you might be sneaking into a field of wheat under cover of darkness, carrying a large plank, only to come to your senses in the nick of time and recognize that you are about to fake an intricate crop circle and are quite probably trespassing on private property.

Forearmed with the correct information is to be fore-warned. Plus, we want you to have a few laughs along the way, which is more than can be said for the poor horse.

CONTENTS

1. TELL IF YOUR NEIGHBOR IS A ZOMBIE:

Nothing brings down property prices in your area quicker than the discovery that you have a reanimated human corpse living next door. Your neighbor seems never to sleep, his lack of free will is alarming to say the least, and his craving for human flesh means you live in constant fear for your life. However, before you run over there with a chain saw, spend a little time observing his movements to make sure that he really is a member of the undead, rather than a Goth or Keith Richards.

WHAT IS A ZOMBIE?

First decide which of the two types of zombie that you are dealing with: Hollywood B-movie zombie or Haitian voodoo zombie. The former is a human corpse that has come back to "life," while the latter has had his free will and "Ti Bon Ange"

(Creole for "little good angel") or soul removed by a sorcerer. To keep things simple, let's assume that you are most likely to be troubled by the Hollywood B-movie strain.

— CHARACTERISTICS —

Zombies enjoy groaning and milling around in groups. Personal hygiene is poor: for example, your neighbor might have an arm hanging off, wear tattered clothing, and reek of rotting flesh. Other tell-tale signs include:

If he could understand the question, "Where do you see yourself in five years time?", he would probably answer "Still feasting on the brains of the living." All other hobbies and interests will have been subsumed by his all-consuming and unquenchable hunger for fresh human flesh

Unresponsive to communication

Pale complexion and clammy skin

Anything less subtle than a baseball bat is unlikely to discourage him from invading your personal space or biting your neck

Dull expression of the eyes

Lumbering gait, often with hands held out in front of the body at arms length

Insensible to pain (for example, he doesn't cry out when you step on his foot, cut off his arm, or try to run him over repeatedly with your car)

HOW TO DESTROY YOUR ZOMBIE NEIGHBOR

If you can't run away or he corners you in an alley with a bunch of his friends, you should either burn or decapitate him. Zombies are highly susceptible to fire or electrocution. It is a common misconception that they have superhuman strength. In fact, their poor agility and coordination make them an easy target for your average flame thrower and/or M79 grenade launcher.

2. STAGE A COUP:

First decide which kind of coup you would like: bloody or bloodless. As the name suggests, a bloody coup involves a lot of blood, ricocheting bullets, looting, and general mayhem. However, a bloodless coup, though bloodless, is no walk in the park. Both types of coup require you to depose the established government quickly and decisively. You can't maneuver yourself into power simply by baking cookies and offering them to the chief of the military (although this helps).

CHOOSE YOUR FRIENDS

If your social life consists of hanging around with your posse outside your local fast-food joint arguing about which DVD you are going to rent that evening, then you need to change your social circle. Before you can even think about staging a coup, you've got to get on a first-name basis with large sections of the armed forces, police, or National Guard. Your biggest drinking buddy should be someone like the chief of the armed forces, or, at the very least, a disaffected member of a government agency with access to a large stash of weapons.

CHOOSE YOUR COUNTRY

You can learn a lot about a country from its proverbs. Which of these two countries do you think is ripe for a coup?

> Motto A: "Money is power."
> Motto B: "Every time a donkey brays,
> it remembers something."

The answer is, of course, B, typically a small Marxist dictatorship with a population of three million subsistence farmers. Country A is most likely an established capitalist democracy. Stay away from democracies, even small struggling ones, as you'll attract lots of unwelcome air strikes from other countries trying to prop up those in power. However, attacking a Marxist dictatorship will not invite Russian or Chinese hostility, so long as you can persuade them that you are pro-Russian or pro-Chinese.

CUT ABOVE THE NECK

Shear off the top layer of government while leaving the old bureaucracy and infrastructure intact but don't do it in haste. For example, if you have arranged for the U.S. Marines to airlift the deposed president out of the country "for his own safety," make sure they do it on the day of the coup. Any earlier looks suspicious.

CONTROL COMMUNICATIONS

After the coup, you must control the flow of information in and out of the country. Seize the broadcast and paper media. Put the airport out of action by placing a bomb, car, or herd of goats in the middle of the runaway.

IT'S A JUGGLING ACT

Convince everyone else in the world that you are pro-them. That means showing democracies that you are pro-democracy (promise to provide for free elections, triple-ply toilet paper, and MTV) while simultaneously persuading autocracies that you are autocratic (free vodka). For example, if your first public act once you're in power is a march past of tanks, karaoke, and cappuccino machines, you will convince everyone that you're the person to be trusted.

3. eBay SCAMS:

There's a whole world of cyber-pain to be dished out to gullible, hasty, and plain stupid eBayers, especially newbies. Here are some of the most popular scams.

BID WITHDRAWAL

Choose an item to bid on that has no bids and no reserve price. Make your first bid $1,000 (it will only show as whatever the opening bid is, which could be as little as $0.01), then use a friend's account to make a second bid for $990. You will then automatically become the highest bidder at $995. Seconds before the end of the auction, withdraw your friend's bid, and the final selling price will revert to the opening bid. The auction then ends, and so long as nobody has sniped you, the seller will be obliged to sell to you at this crazily low price.

IMPROVE YOUR FEEDBACK

Set up an account and sell lots of cheap products quickly, and mail them efficiently, so that you get lots of good feedback. Then list several expensive items. Anyone who sees your feedback and looks no further can be taken for a sucker. Take their money (using Western Union, checks, or postal orders) and disappear.

HIJACK A SELLER ACCOUNT

Send a phishing email to ask an unsuspecting eBay user with a dormant account to update their account details. Ask them to confirm their user ID and passwords, then you can steal their account and use their good feedback to set up some fake auctions with high value items.

SHAMEFUL POSTAGE

Sell an item cheaply but charge very high postage to catch impulse buyers unaware. Lots of eBayers in the Far East use this method to sell cheap trinkets for a few dollars but charge $40 for delivery. Claim that the package is coming from Hong Kong even though you live two blocks away from your buyer.

THE WESTERN UNION SCAM

Sell an expensive item like a laptop at a cut price (to encourage more takers). Use Western Union for the money transfer but send nothing. You can pick up the money at any Western Union worldwide and disappear.

FEEDBACK BOMBING

Use multiple eBay user IDs to deliberately damage another eBayer's account by leaving multiple negative feedbacks. Due to feedback bombing, the victim will probably have to register a new eBay account.

FREE ITEMS

Sell a "foolproof program" which promises to unlock a world of free gifts and samples. Then send successful bidders a plan advising them to pretend they are a business and to request free samples from many different manufacturers and wholesalers (this is fraud).

WHOLESALE LIST SCAM

List an expensive item at a bargain price, show photos, and give all the item's specifications. Then somewhere in the item description mention that you are selling a wholesale list only (a worthless list of wholesalers) from which they can buy their item. They get what they paid for, even though many buyers will believe they are bidding on the actual item, and will have little recourse for not reading the small print.

BUY AND SWITCH

Purchase two identical items, one broken and the other in good working order. When the sound item arrives, claim it was damaged in the post and send back the old item. Watch out for serial numbers and identification stickers on electrical goods.

4. BEAT A SPEED CAMERA:

Every year millions of people get fined for speeding. This puts points on their licenses and increases their motor insurance. These fines generate tens of millions of dollars and do little to make the roads safer (since everyone now drives with one eye watching the side of the road to check for speed cameras and brakes heavily when they spot one). Fortunately there are several ways to beat them.

SPRAY-ON PROTECTION

The majority of red light and speed cameras use a strong flash to photograph your license plate. Photo-Blocker comes in a can: you spray it on your plate to produce a high-powered gloss that reflects the light back towards the camera, so that your plate appears overexposed and white on the photo. It is easy to apply and the manufacturers claim that one application is good for at least two years, although you have to polish and wax the plate regularly to maintain a good shine.

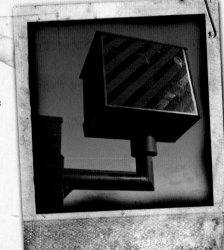

NAVALERT

Invest in one of the many red light and speed camera detectors on the market. Powered by a cigar lighter, they sit on your dashboard and make timely announcements such as "camera ahead limit 60." This gives you plenty of time to slow down and drive like a model citizen. If you don't slow down, you'll even be warned that you are going too fast. You can keep the software up to date via the Internet, by checking on what new cameras are being used, and which ones have been removed. Most devices will also warn you when you are approaching high collision areas and schools, thus improving road safety without you having to part with your cash.

WARP SPEED

There is a popular myth that says if you go fast enough through a speed camera it won't react quickly enough to take your picture. The British motoring show Top Gear put this theory to the test. First, the camera clocked a Honda Civic Type-R doing 129 mph. Then a Mercedes CL55 was driven past at 148 mph and was also caught. However, a TVR Tuscan S screamed past the camera at 171 mph without being detected. Conclusion: it's technically possible, but probably not worth the risk or the expense of buying a high-performance sports car.

BEATING THE TICKET

If you do get caught speeding, you can still beat the ticket:

1. Selective amnesia is your friend. When the speeding fine arrives in the mail, fire back a letter saying you need to see photo proof, because you can't establish who was driving. If they can't identify who was behind the wheel, they can't make you pay.

2. Send a check for a few dollars more than the fine. The system will send you a check back for the difference, but don't cash it. You won't lose demerit points from your license until the financial transaction is complete, so if you tear up the check, it will never happen (this sounds plausible but is probably an urban myth! Still worth a try, though).

Finally, if you really want to beat the system, here's a radical idea you may not have tried yet: don't drive faster than the speed limit.

5. BECOME A MAFIA BOSS:

Just as you would be unwise to attempt to hang someone upside down and then carve them till they bleed without first locating a sturdy ceiling beam, you'd be absolutely crazy to consider founding your own Mafia dynasty until you own a string of casinos and brothels, and are deeply involved in money laundering, extortion, drugs, and prostitution. Since the only people who are in that position are already Mafia dons, it begs the question, which came first: the chicken or the cement shoes? In short, the only way to become the next John Gotti is to work your way up from the bottom of a prominent crime family. Yep, it's the same corporate grind whatever career you choose (unless you luck out and land a job at Google—seriously, those guys have gourmet staff restaurants, free laundry, and a petting zoo).

If you do choose a life of crime, remember that the Mafia is not just about guns, money, decapitating horses, and killing people. Being part of the Mafia is a big responsibility to take on. You have to earn trust and respect.

LOCATION, LOCATION, LOCATION

As a member of a criminal fraternity, you will be expected to travel, but you should pick one of these three cities as your base:

LAS VEGAS: Sin City is the gambling center of the world (OK, not counting Macao, which has just overtaken it in terms of total gambling revenue. You want to run the show and didn't know that?). A recent crackdown on organized crime by law enforcement means that other criminal gangs apart from the Mafia have risen to prominence, so you've got even more chance of getting wasted by your rivals. However, with hot summers, mild winters, and abundant year-round sunshine, few places can match up.

NEW YORK: It's got great restaurants and theater, and is home to the big five U.S. crime families: Bonanno, Colombo, Genovese, Gambino, and Lucchese. If you seek the authentic Godfather meets The Sopranos experience, this is the place to go.

CHICAGO: The family in the Windy City, generally known as the "Outfit," has ruled organized crime in the city since the end of Prohibition. It is home to Al Capone, one of the most famous gangsters who ever lived, and is the single greatest symbol of the collapse of law and order in the United States during the 1920s.

START BREAKING THE LAW

Start with petty theft, stealing cars, and dealing drugs, or, if you are a nerd, start hacking and doing internet scams (electronic crime is BIG business). Your criminal activities will soon attract the attention of the local gang leader (usually a guy called "Fat Tony"). He'll offer to cut you up bad if you don't join his gang, and he'll invite you to shoot someone in a restaurant or dump a body in the river to show that you mean business. Don't mess this up; there's an old Italian saying: "You screw up once, you lose two teeth."

OTHER ESSENTIALS

Learn how to drive, swing a baseball bat, and shoot people (known in criminal circles as "popping a cap up yo ass"). Buy a pair of shades and an 8x10 photo of Frank Sinatra for your nightstand. Always wear shoes with pointy ends and a white hat with a wide black rim, and kiss people Mediterranean style (three cheeks).

6. BECOME A PORN STAR:

Girls have an easier time getting into porn than men. If you're a woman with a nice face and body (a 6 or above on the 1 to 10 scale), then you can go to Los Angeles for a week and make two movies a day if you want, then go home with a wad of cash. Guys, on the other hand, have to live in Los Angeles and either be very attractive with a great body, or know someone (a female porn actress, director who wants to work with you, a crew member, etc.) who can get you into a movie.

WHAT QUALITIES DO I NEED?

For a girl, apart from a hot body, you need to be able to deliver a hot performance every time. For a guy, you've got to be able to keep wood and "release" on cue.

Also, you'll need the universal qualities that help people in any job—have a good attitude, don't bring your personal problems to work, and be fairly disciplined. No employer likes unreliability.

DOES SIZE MATTER?

If you're a guy you don't need a huge cock. At least five inches is good, and a couple more is even better, because the camera needs to see some shaft during penetration.

HOW MUCH MONEY SHOULD I ASK FOR?

When you're starting off, you may get as little as $100 per scene. Then it's up to you to work hard and climb the porno ladder of success. If you get a reputation for being hot and good to work with, more lucrative offers will come your way.

Generally, girls make more than guys. Girls make between $300 to $2,000 per sex scene, depending on what type of sex is involved. If she's high-profile, like a Playboy Playmate, she'll get top dollar. Guys make about half as much as girls, and their rate is generally the same, regardless of what type of sex they are performing. For a magazine shoot, guys and girls usually get $500 to $800. Once you've done a few magazine shoots, you can raise your movie rate.

SHOULD I GET AN AGENT?

There are a few good agents and lots of bad ones. Get a friend in the business to recommend a good one. If you get an agent, they can tell you which porno companies to avoid and which ones will treat you well, plus they can negotiate your fee.

CAN I CONTROL THE TYPE OF WORK?

You can decide what you will and won't do—but clearly the more you do, the more money you'll get. You'll have little control over the projects unless you hire your own film crew and photographer. This is expensive, but the upside of running the show yourself is that you get a bigger slice of the royalties, rather than a one-off flat fee.

WHAT ABOUT THE INTERNET?

It's a great way to get your wares out to a potentially limitless amount of customers. Get a friend to design a web site, upload your photos and you're in business. Try www.webdesignadult.com; it's a high end design firm specializing in custom adult websites geared towards generating guaranteed revenues.

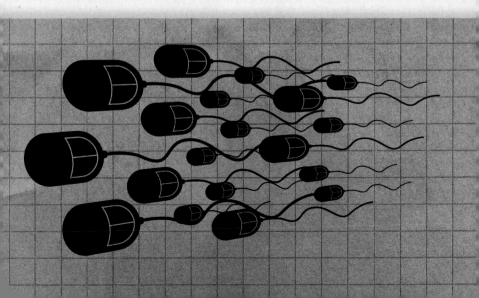

7. THE CORRECT WAY TO GIVE SOMEONE A NOOGIE:

The world of pain that is widely referred to by the endearingly euphemistic epithet "noogie" involves trapping a person in a headlock, swiftly followed by the rubbing of a knuckle, fist, or hand on the scalp, with the intention of causing pain, hair displacement, and mild humiliation.

Do you know how to deliver one correctly? Just because you're a stereotypical dumb jock whose been doling them out for as long as you can remember doesn't mean that you are doing it right.

THE APPROACH

Soon after you select your victim from the other end of a high school corridor, your brain stem will send a signal to your knuckle that a noogie is imminent. Several seconds later the same message will arrive at your legs, which will begin to propel your 260-pound frame toward them.

ESTABLISH EYE CONTACT

In primates, the unwavering gaze has evolved as a sign of dominance and threat. Initiate eye-to-eye contact, and smile inanely as you continue to lumber forward. This allows your myopic prey ample opportunity to appreciate the flawless inevitability of the phalangeal-cranial synergy that is about to occur.

THE HEADLOCK

If you are right-handed, clamp your victim's head in the crook of your left elbow while simultaneously making a fist with your right hand, with the knuckle of your middle finger standing proud. Look around to solicit peer approval from your Pleistocene Epoch teammates as you drill hard into the top of your victim's head.

Just as rubbing a balloon causes a build-up of charged particles on your body, this grinding action actually encourages the flow of positive "grade-point-average" energy between you and your victim. It won't make you a valedictorian, but it might stimulate some of your automatic brain functions such as breathing, temperature control, and heart rate. If not, follow up with a nipple twist and a Chinese burn.

8. BUILD AN ATOM BOMB:

Whatever you do, don't tell anyone that you are assembling a nuclear device in your garage. A single indiscreet moment down at the bar can land you in big trouble.

BEG, BORROW, AND STEAL

First obtain several pounds of weapons grade plutonium, or two sub-critical masses of uranium 235. This is the easy part. The stuff is lying around all over the place in the ex-Soviet Union. Take a trip there, and if you can't find any in the

children's play area of the nearest municipal park, then you will easily be able to bribe a technician in the nuclear industry.

Smuggling it back home is the tricky part. Either bribe a diplomat, who can smuggle it into the country in their lead-lined diplomatic pouch, or hide it in your check-in luggage and hope that the security staff at the airport are having yet another one of their off days.

Explosive Device

Gunpowder

Uranium 235

ASSEMBLING THE DEVICE

Once you get your nuclear fissile material safely home, you need to construct a means of colliding two lumps of the stuff at high speed, to create a nuclear chain reaction. This is the same principle that was used for the Hiroshima bomb—essentially you need to make a double-ended firework. Wear protective clothing, and if at any time you feel nauseous or your hair begins to fall out, seek medical advice immediately.

Get a nine-foot-long piece of metal drain piping and drill several small holes in it at regular intervals. Weld several small lengths of copper pipe onto these holes, then cover the drain pipe in concrete, leaving all the ends (copper and pipe) exposed. The copper pipes act as vent holes, so that the initial explosion doesn't splinter the pipe and send radioactive isotopes in all directions.

Pack each end of the pipe with a generous lump of the nuclear material along with a few pounds of plastic explosive. Rig both sets of explosive up to a detonator and a timer. This can be a simple VCR timer, or better still, a mobile phone set to vibrate. Then you can phone the device from anywhere in the world to detonate the bomb.

You will greatly increase the efficiency of the bomb if you can get your hands on a directional thermal neutron emitter. If not, don't worry about it. Just seal the ends of the pipe by welding metal bungs onto them and then cover with more concrete.

THE EFFECTS OF THE BOMB

If you detonate the device at ground level, you will flatten everything within a mile, but the real destruction will be caused by the nuclear fallout, as radioactive debris blows high into the air and spreads for hundreds of miles, killing thousands of people and making the surrounding area uninhabitable for years to come.

9. NEGOTIATE WITH KIDNAPPERS:

Governments always say: "Don't negotiate with kidnappers. To do so would only invite more." We don't know about you, but most people given $5 million and an Aston Martin DB7 as a getaway vehicle would have to be a workaholic or in a whole lot of debt not to call it a day. Even after you've given 40 percent to your accomplice in the police force, you've still got enough to buy a Pacific island retreat. So, the take-home message is: start the negotiations.

Here are six tips for negotiating the release of your loved ones:

1. If the kidnappers are international terrorists (rather than local crooks) and you live in Japan, Italy, or France, you can open a bottle of champagne now. Your government will have handed over a large wad of unmarked bills before you even knew that your loved one was missing.

2. If you live in the U.S. or U.K., the protocol is more protracted. They will publicly claim no deal, while selling them truckloads of stinger missiles in

exchange for drug money which can then be used to fund anticommunist rebels in Central America.

3. There's no better place to cut your teeth as a negotiator than in Mexico, the kidnapping capital of the world. Official figures show less than 300 kidnappings a year, but the reality is more like ten times that figure. They go unreported because many of the perpetrators are high ranking policemen or ex-policemen. Increasingly, people from middle-income families are becoming the most lucrative victims. So take a vacation to Mexico and you can get in some negotiating practice while you are there.

4. Try to identify the general whereabouts of the hostage. Obviously, if you knew the precise location you could send in your own crack team of privately hired ex-special forces guys, but if you know at least which city or country is holding them you can then make approaches to influential figures around the city or area.

5. Keep the kidnappers on the phone. The more talking they do, the less chance they'll cut off an ear or behead someone. Kidnappers are terrible at multitasking. That's why they always sound so stressed.

10. BULLFIGHT:

The Spanish call it corrida de toros; Hemingway called it a grand passion, "the only art in which the artist is in danger of death." Bullfighters need skill, courage, and a Ph.D. in bull psychology.

Bullfighting is a ritual that plays out in specific prearranged steps. First, you and your team enter the arena in a parade, or paseíllo, accompanied by band music. Line up in scar order: the oldest matador goes to the far left, while the newest walks in the middle. You'll be wearing a figure-hugging sequined suit called a traje de luces (literally, a suit of lights), and if you're new to the Plaza, you won't be wearing your hat. The bullfight is divided into the following three main parts (tercios):

TERCIO DE VARAS ("LANCES THIRD")

The bull charges into the ring. He is at least four years old, weighs about half a ton, and he's pissed. He is tested for ferocity by you (the matador) and "trained" to follow and attack the cape. The two picadors mounted on horseback impale the bull in its neck with lances. If they throw the lances hard enough they embed themselves so far that the lever effect breaks some of the bull's ribs.

It's your job to execute a series of impressive maneuvers with a very heavy magenta and gold dress cape called a capote. These maneuvers allow you to learn about the bull's behavior, such as whether it charges in straight or curved lines, or whether it has any defects such as eyesight problems or a clubbed foot. You must perform a number of fundamental passes with the cape. The closer you can get the bull to pass by your body, the better. The basic pass, from which all the others spring, is called the "Veronica" in which the cape is drawn over the bull's head while you strike a pose.

TERCIO DE BANDERILLAS ("BANDERILLAS THIRD")

Three banderilleros each attempt to plant two brightly-colored barbed sticks (banderillas, literally "little flags") on the bull's flanks causing major loss of blood, and further weakening the animal. You can sit this one out and save your energy for the finale.

TERCIO DE MUERTE ("DEATH THIRD")

You re-enter the ring alone with a small red cape in one hand and a thirty-three-inch-long sword in the other. Even though the bull is weakened, he is now at his most dangerous. You execute another set of crowd-pleasing passes, and if you are really daring, you kneel in front of the bull. They love that. After an impressive pass, look at the crowd, puff out your chest and shout, "Quién es el papá?" (Who's the daddy?). You've got to flaunt it.

Before the kill, dedicate the animal to an individual by handing them your hat (montero), or place your hat on the ground to dedicate the bull to everyone. Kill the bull cleanly and efficiently with style and in a way that exposes you to maximum danger. The act of thrusting the sword is called an estocada. For the best kill, the estocada recibido, allow the bull to charge you while you stand your ground, then thrust the sword between the shoulder blades (a target about the size of your palm). When performed correctly, the bull will expire within minutes. If the crowd really loves you, you'll be rewarded with one or two ears and the tail. Screw it up and you'll be booed and showered with cushions.

11. HAVE FUN IN AN ELEVATOR:

Elevators are designed with one purpose in mind: to transport people up and down quickly, safely, and efficiently. What a boring world it would be if everything had just a single purpose. That's why every elevator has a second purpose: to trap unsuspecting victims in a confined space with YOU. Just imagine the possibilities. Here are a few choice elevator pranks.

THE POWER OF SIGNS

The general public pays far too much attention to signage than is good for them, which makes for more fun for you. Stick a sign below the call button which says "Obese individuals are strictly prohibited from using the elevators." Then hide nearby and watch how fat and gullible someone has to be to obey it. If you want to be more direct and straightforward with your signage just write: "USE THE STAIRS, LARDASS."

Alternatively, print a sign which says "Caution Elevator Broken, DO NOT USE! Press emergency button for assistance" and tape it to the inside of the sliding doors, so that it will only be visible when the doors close. Then hide and listen for the screams and sirens. If you are feeling really cruel, print a sign saying "Frayed elevator cable. Use at your own risk."

SCREAM

Get into a crowded elevator and then scream just as the doors are closing. The reaction from the other people around you is hilarious.

DARE TO BE DIFFERENT

You know how everyone faces the same way in an elevator? That's because the urge to conform is so strong. Face the other way and see how quickly people become irritated or

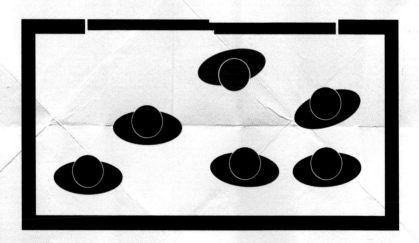

uneasy because they think you're being antisocial (which you kind of are, you freakazoid).

BE ANNOYINGLY NICE

Keep letting people on the elevator until it is full. Repeat this at every floor; keep stopping the doors to allow just one more person on. You're being so damn nice that other people will find it hard to tell you to stop, so they'll have to seethe in silence.

WHEN YOU'VE GOT TO GO

This one is more elaborate: get an old toilet bowl and a paper holder. Stick the paper holder to the wall, then sit on the toilet inside the elevator with your pants down and wait for someone to open the doors. This works best on those old-fashioned elevators with hinged doors that you have to open yourself. Most people will say sorry and close the door again to give you the privacy you deserve!

12. MAKE A WATER BOMB:

This is the only bomb you can get caught with without getting hauled off to another country for interrogation. Yes folks, the water bomb is one of the most ancient antisocial uses of the wet stuff in the civilized world, ranking just below signing your name in fresh snow. Sure, a balloon can hold more, but the self-sufficiency of the origami method is deeply satisfying.

1. Take a piece of letter-size paper. Fold one of the corners across to the opposite edge and cut off the extra strip so that you are left with a square. Now make a crease between the other two corners, and a further two creases by making opposite sides meet. Now you've got four creases, which meet in the center of the square, and when you stand it on its base it will look like a 3D four-pointed star.

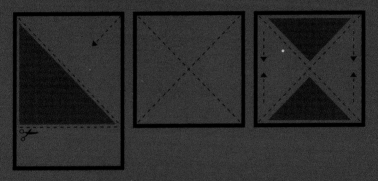

2. Turn the 3D star into a 2D triangle by closing up two opposite sides. Then fold in all four loose corners into the apex to make a small diamond.

3. Fold in the left and right points of the diamond, then turn over and repeat.

4. Tuck each of the four points at the long end of this hexagon into its corresponding little pouch, which has been formed by folding in the points of the diamond in the last step. Fold them down to make them stay in their pouches.

5. Blow through the hole in the top, and you now have a hollow cube just begging to be filled with water and then lobbed at someone you've got a huge crush on in the misguided hope that somehow your clumsy prepubescent assault will be interpreted as courtship. How can the object of your affection fail to appreciate the fruits of your craftsmanship, or see you as anything less than a giant in the field of handcrafted liquid-payload projectiles?

13. PERFORM OPEN HEART SURGERY:

Open heart surgery is often cited as one of the most invasive of all medical procedures, requiring expertise of the highest level for a successful outcome. But hey, it's not brain surgery. Here's how to fix a simple case of stenotic arteriosclerotic coronary artery disease in ten steps, and with no previous medical knowledge (allow between three to four hours for the operation).

1. Before you begin, familiarize yourself with the anatomy of the heart. In brief, it has a right and left ventricle, and a right and left atrium. The right ventrical pumps oxygen-poor blood into the lungs, and the left ventrical pumps oxygen-rich blood to the rest of the body . . . yawn . . . and swiftly on . . .

2. Scrub up. This involves making urbane conversation with your colleagues while washing your hands with yellow soap, and skillfully operating stainless steel taps with your elbows.

Bypass Graft

Left Coronary
Artery

Blocked Artery

3. The bit before the operation is called Pre-Op. Give the patient a sedative in his arm to keep him calm and to reduce the risk that he'll ask you any tough questions, like "Can I see some ID?" Shave and scrub the patient's chest area to reduce the risk of infection. Finally, make sure you have an anaesthetist (who puts the patient to sleep) and a perfusionist (who is responsible for the oxygenation of the blood). Basically, they keep the patient alive while you get to do all the fun stuff.

4. Once the patient is unconscious, cut open the leg and grab a piece of the saphenous vein. You'll need this later to create the bypass.

5. Make an incision down the center of the patient's chest, then crank open the breastbone with a sternal retractor.

6. Slice down the middle of the pericardium, the membranous sac which contains the heart.

7. Get one of the nurses to mop your brow.

8. Make two slits in the coronary artery wall above and below the blockage, then carefully sew the leg vessel graft onto the coronary artery using very fine synthetic sutures. Repeat steps 7 and 8, depending on how many grafts are required.

9. Attach temporary pacemaker wires to the right and left atrium; this will be used during the patient's recovery to correct any irregular heartbeats.

10. Insert a chest drain to remove excess fluid, stitch up the chest, and then send out for pizza. The patient should remain in the intensive care unit (ICU) for one to two days, then in the hospital for another five days for monitoring.

14. COUNT CARDS AT A CASINO:

Card counting is the only way you can statistically improve your chances of winning at the blackjack table, but then only by a few percent. In the film *Rain Man*, Dustin Hoffman's character memorizes an eight deck shoe, but in real life, you don't have to be an autistic savant with a photographic memory to use a card counting system, of which there are hundreds, but we will discuss the most common.

GOLDEN RULE: DON'T GET CAUGHT.

Counting cards isn't illegal, so long as you use your brain and not an electronic device. However, that doesn't mean that a casino will tolerate you if they suspect you of counting. Many casinos are private property, so they can throw you out without giving a reason and charge you with trespassing if you return. In some joints, the dealers count too, and shuffle the pack when the odds swing in your favor. Many casinos use eight deck shoes and prohibit mid-shoe entry, which means that you can't just join when the decks are looking good.

When you play blackjack, certain cards favor the dealer and other cards favor the player. Very simply, the more high cards left in the shoe, the better the player's chances of winning, because a dealer must hit if he has less than 17. But you don't have to remember every single card that has been played; you just need to keep a running tally of hi versus lo cards.

THE HI/LO SYSTEM

Ace	2	3	4	5	6	7	8	9	10	Jack	Queen	King
-1	+1	+1	+1	+1	+1	0	0	0	-1	-1	-1	-1

As each card is dealt, add or subtract 1 from your running total. The higher the total, the better your odds and the more you bet; zero means it's 50-50; and a negative number means the dealer has the advantage.

So, if the deal is A, 8, 5, 2, 9, K, J, then the running total will be -1, -1, 0, +1, +1, 0, -1. However, you also have to divide the running total by the number of decks of cards still in the shoe to get a true count.

BET SPREAD

This means betting high when your chances are good and low when they are not. For instance, you may bet $80 on good hands and $10 on low. However, in light of the golden rule, if you make the bet spread (the difference between your big and small bets) too obvious (i.e., more than 8 to 1), you may get invited to a backroom beating.

USE THIS TABLE AS
A ROUGH BET SPREAD GUIDE:

True Count	Betting Units
+1	1
+2 or +3	2
+4 or +5	3
+6 or +7	4
+8 or +9	5

Be patient and try to look like a tourist or a loser gambler bum rather than a card-counting newbie. Counting cards will not make you a millionaire overnight. The glory days of card counting are long gone anyway, because the casinos have made the game more difficult to beat by increasing the number of decks, limiting bet spreads, and capping bets. You could make more money by getting yourself an evening job in a 7-11 or pumping gas.

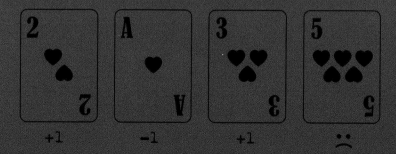

15. SCREW UP SOMEONE'S CAR:

There are too many cars on the road, so screwing over an enemy's vehicle is good for you and the environment. Fortunately, there are lots of subtle and not-so-subtle ways to mess with their engine without having to take a baseball bat to the paintwork, which is time consuming and wakes up the neighbors. Here are a few quieter solutions and a sweet myth exploded.

SUGAR IN THE GAS TANK

We've all heard of this one. The sugar is supposed to dissolve in the gas and then caramelize once it reaches the pistons. The trouble is, sugar isn't soluble in gas, so all it really does is clog up the fuel filter and starve the engine of air. It will definitely cause problems, but is unlikely to total the engine. A better solution is to pour diesel into the tank of a gasoline car. This will wreck the engine. Pouring regular gas into a diesel engine won't destroy it, but will require the tank to be drained, which should cost at least $150.

OIL TROUBLE

Drain the oil from the oil pan. The car will seize up within minutes and destroy the engine. However, unless you cut the wires leading to the gauges, a warning light will come on to say there's no oil. So replace the oil with very thin oil, like two-cycle oil. This will cause engine damage without tripping the oil light. Alternatively, leave the oil intact but replace the oil drain plug with a cork. Once the car has warmed up, the crankcase pressure will blow the cork and oil out very quickly, causing lots of damage before the warning light comes on.

CAVITY WALL FILLER

Drill a small hole in the window and pump in a large can of expanding foam filler which grows to thirty times the dispensed amount and hardens within minutes.

STYRENE SOLUTION

Pouring a pint of styrene (autobody resin) in the crankcase will make the engine lock up tight within a hundred miles.

FRUIT AND VEGETABLES

Make sure your victim gets at least one of his five portions of fruits and veggies—up his exhaust pipe. Ram it in hard with a broom handle and a mechanic will have to strip down half the engine before he finds the fault.

RICER SELF-DESTRUCTION

If your victim is a ricer (a dumb ass who makes unnecessary modifications to their—most often imported Japanese—car to make it look like it goes faster), then the easiest way to screw up his car is to give him $1,000 and let him destroy it himself with unnecessary performance mods. Next time you see him, he'll have a ten-inch exhaust tip, incorrect badging, seat harnesses, offset tape stripes, a single wiper conversion, and an oversized fiberglass bodykit. One speed bump and he'll crash into a tree.

If none of the above appeals to you, steal the car, drive it to an upper-class suburb, and set it on fire.

16. BREAK INTO A CAR:

There are two groups of people who break into cars. In the first group are career criminals who spray paint the car, remove the engine block security numbers, change the plates, and sell it. People in this group already know how to break into cars. So if you're reading this, you must be part of the second group: you're a twelve-year-old joyriding punk who didn't get enough attention when you were little. Hi kid. Did you steal this book too?

Here's what you do:

1. Only break into a car with an automatic transmission, since you probably can't drive a manual. The downside is that an automatic is more likely to have a car alarm.

2. Any car with a flashing light on or near the dash has a car alarm, so move on. Any car with a light on top of the roof is a cop car. You definitely don't want to steal that.

3. You can learn a lot about the driver by looking at the seat. If it is set low and pulled back with a big butt-sized indent in it, you know the car is driven by a 250-pound steroid-popping freak who will rip your arms off if he catches you. Choose a car with the seat forward and high—it's probably driven by a woman.

4. If you just want to joyride rather than sell the car, hammer a large flathead screwdriver in the keyhole and turn hard (this should break the pins and allow you to turn the chamber). Or use a lock-out tool kit.

5. Bring a cushion with you; even when you've raised the seat as far as it will go, you'll still need it to help you see over the steering wheel.

6. To start the car, if you've got a manufacturer's key, use that, otherwise on older models you can splice the two red wires underneath or inside the dash, or stick a screw hammer into the ignition and pop it out, then use a screwdriver to turn the brass triangle.

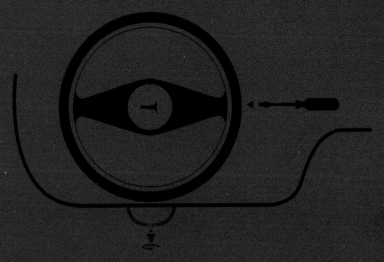

7. Use your seatbelt. That way, when the cops start chasing you and you wrap the car around a tree, you'll walk away with your life. You've got a bright future ahead of you. In five years, you should be clearing $3,000 a week dealing drugs, so don't mess it up by getting wasted too early.

17. SHOPLIFT:

You don't need us to tell you that shoplifting is a criminal act, but we should also draw your attention to the morality of screwing over the big boys like Wal-Mart and Target versus hitting the small independent shops. That's a matter for your own conscience.

RECON MISSION

It's a good idea to check out a store before you actually steal anything from it. This allows you to locate the surveillance cameras and to work out where the blind spots are. On this visit, buy a couple of small inexpensive items so you look like a regular shopper. Beware of mirrors on the walls at corners as they usually have cameras in them. Check out the obesity of the security guard. Ideally, he should be morbidly obese and incapable of chasing you without popping an artery. Beware the little scrawny guards; not only are they quick on their feet, but they also have more to prove.

GO SOLO

Nothing is more suspicious than a group of three or four shoplifters, especially if they are teenagers. Go alone but make sure you've got a getaway driver outside with the engine running. Walk into the store casually and greet the door greeter. His or her job is to make you feel welcome, but also to make potential shoplifters feel noticed, because thieves thrive on anonymity. But you're a regular shopper, right, so don't let this phase you. Remember the odds are in your favor: in the U.S., as many as one in twelve customers is a shoplifter, and each one commits an average of fifty thefts before being caught.

HAVE A PURPOSE

If you walk into a shop with the sole aim of stealing something, it will show. So you need to buy a few specific (but cheap) items, so that you don't raise suspicion by wandering aimlessly around the store. Always have enough money in your wallet to pay for the stolen items as well, so that if you get caught you can burst into tears and say it was a one-time thing and offer to pay (tell them your mother just died and this is your way of grieving). Pick up your target item, along with some of your smaller things, then walk to a camera blind spot, pocket it, and then take something from the shelf to show you have an innocent reason for being there.

TRUST YOUR INSTINCT

If at any time you get a bad feeling, trust your instinct. Accept that today is an off day and put the stuff back. Walk out of the shop. Even if you get stopped, you can't be arrested if you haven't taken stuff off the premises. If you have stolen something and the alarm sounds at the exit, keep walking. They can only stop and search you if they have actually seen you steal. They can't lay a finger on you otherwise, so keep walking and threaten legal action if anyone tries to detain you, because they aren't cops.

18. SAW A WOMAN IN HALF:

There are many ways of sawing a woman in half. Some magicians use chainsaws, others use rotary saws. In this explanation, all you need is a large handsaw and a person-sized box made of a soft wood that is easy to cut through. Don't make the box too thick or you'll run out of energy before you're finished.

1. Your assistant steps into the empty crate and lies down on her back.

2. You place the lid on top and nail it down.

3. Saw through the middle of the crate until you reach about halfway (you could replace the wood in the center of the crate with strips of insulation board to make it easier to saw through).

4. Stop and pull the saw out and make a big deal of how tired you are and that you need to take a rest.

5. Place the saw back into the groove from the side (not from the top). The reason for this is that while you were "resting," your assistant has arched her back, so that when you replace the saw it is now underneath her body (she can help to guide the saw).

6. Keep sawing until you reach the bottom of the box. It will fall open to reveal an intact assistant.

7. If you are doing this on the street, now is the time to pass around the hat. Collect as much money as you can, then split before the crowd figures out how easily you've tricked them.

19. THROW A PUNCH:

So, you're an ambidextrous fighter—you get knocked out with either hand, huh? Then chances are you need to go back to basics and learn to pack a punch.

MAKE A FIST

The key to delivering a world of pain without breaking your hand or wrist is to form a fist correctly. Lots of Friday-night brawlers mistakenly curl their fingers around their thumb. Listen for the crack: it's your thumb, not the other guy's nose. The thumb should be outside the fist, wrapped around and across the rest of the fingers, but not sticking out further than the first joint (you're trying to lay someone out, not hitch a ride). Also keep your fist in line with the wrist and arm. Bending at the wrist is just another shortcut to the ER.

SQUARE UP

An effective punch begins with a good stance. You can either stand facing your opponent, with both feet planted shoulder width apart and bent a little at the knees, or turn your body sideways so that the punching arm and its corresponding leg are in line, making you a smaller target to hit.

In boxing, your hands begin in a guard position, with both fists raised to protect your face. In some martial arts, both fists start at your hips, with the elbow pointing backwards and the thumb facing upwards—in Kendo it's called the horse stance. From this position you drive the punching fist forward and rotate it 180 degrees upon impact to inflict maximum soft tissue damage. Meanwhile, the other elbow is driven backwards to increase the power of the punch. Only try this if you have the big guns to back it up—there's nothing more embarrassing than going all Bruce Lee and then getting your ass kicked.

OPEN A CAN

In both boxing and martial arts, the fist travels in a straight line from its starting position and aims for a point half a foot behind the target (usually face or solar plexus). The punch also needs to be fast. The quicker you can deliver the punch, the greater your whooping ability.

Breathe out sharply as you punch. This increases the power and reduces the chance of you being winded if you take one in the stomach. Try to ensure the first two knuckles of the hand connect first. Don't lean into the punch; this makes your head a target and puts you off balance. Keep your feet firmly planted as you strike.

PUT TOGETHER A COMBO

After landing a devastating blow to your opponent's chin or solar plexus, bring back the fist quickly, so that you are ready to throw another and to prevent them from grabbing your arm. A combination of three or four punches is much more effective than a single punch. Don't punch and then wait to see if it has had any effect (there's no turn-taking here). Keep striking at different targets (head, chest, stomach, etc.) until you know you are out of danger.

KEEP PRACTICING

The only way to build speed and power and to make punching second nature is to practice (if you have to think about it, you'll be on the floor getting kicked before you can land a second hit). Practice either on a punching bag or in the air, and if you're a newbie puncher you can improve tenfold in no time at all.

20. PLAY RUSSIAN ROULETTE:

Russian roulette is thought to have been invented by depressive Tsarist officers in the Russian army around 1917. On a wet afternoon when daytime television fails to hold your attention and you are beginning to question your own existence, playing a few rounds can be quite a blast.

HEALTH WARNING

Do not under any circumstances use a semiautomatic pistol. If there is a single round in the magazine, there is a 100 percent chance that it will fire. Even if the magazine is removed, there may still be one bullet in the barrel (on February 28, 2000, a nineteen-year-old man from Houston, Texas, made this mistake, and used a .45-caliber semiautomatic pistol for Russian roulette, unaware that his chances of survival were zero)..

REPEAT—SPIN SUDDEN DEATH

The referee places a round in one of the six chambers of a revolver and spins the cylinder quickly. While it is still spinning, he slaps it sharply back into the body of the gun. If the cylinder is spun inside the body of the gun, the gun should be pointed downwards, otherwise the weight of the bullet tends to make the cylinder come to rest with the bullet toward the bottom, increasing the odds that when the trigger is pulled the hammer will be in contact with an empty chamber (or if you're using a gun like a Mateba Autorevolver, which fires the round in the lower position, you'll greatly increase your risk of being killed).

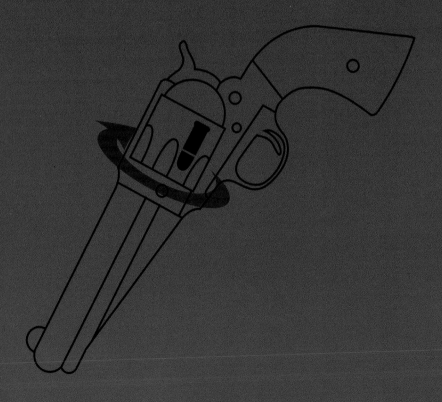

The air should be thick with cigar smoke and crystal meth, and to increase the tension the onlookers will be screaming at each other while waving their wads of cash.

The first player places the gun to his forehead and pulls the trigger. He has just under a 17 percent chance of being killed, which is poor odds compared to most regulated wagering games, especially considering that lives are at risk (for example, in casino craps games, the house pays out 98 percent of what it takes).

The referee spins the cylinder again and hands the gun to the second player who puts it to his forehead and pulls the trigger. The game continues until someone blows their brains out.

SINGLE-SPIN SUDDEN DEATH

In this variation, there are six players and the cylinder is spun only once, at the beginning. The odds of the first player being killed are 6 to 1. However, if the first four players survive, the odds of player five being killed becomes 2 to 1. If he survives, player six is guaranteed to die, either by his own hand, or shot by incensed bystanders when he tries to escape. However, at the start of the game, the sixth player has the greatest odds of surviving, so pick this position if you are given a choice.

21. BEAT A LIE DETECTOR TEST:

The best way to beat the test is to refuse to take one. Even if your employer demands it, it is illegal for them to sack you if you refuse. If your polygraph is for a criminal investigation, your refusal is generally inadmissible in court. However, with a potential employer, you have no choice but to get hooked up to a polygraph if you want the job. In this case, your best weapon is the knowledge that these tests are fallible.

AN INEXACT SCIENCE

Former FBI Supervisory Special Agent Dr. Drew C. Richardson has described polygraph screening as "completely without any theoretical foundation" and, he says, "has absolutely no validity . . . the diagnostic value of this type of testing is no more than that of astrology or tea-leaf reading." In other words, polygraphs frequently produce incorrect results.

HOW THE TEST WORKS

The examiner will ask you three types of question: irrelevant, relevant, and control. An example of an irrelevant
question is "What is your name?" or "What color is your shirt?"
A relevant question pertains to the issue in question: "Did
you steal the money?" or "Have you ever taken illicit drugs?"
These questions will elicit an emotional response, such as
raised blood pressure, pulse, sweat response, and breathing, all of which are measured by the polygraph machine. This
response will be compared to readings taken when you answer
the control questions. These will induce a mild emotional
response but aren't relevant to the investigation, such as
"Have you ever lied to your parents?" or "Have you broken the
speed limit this week?"

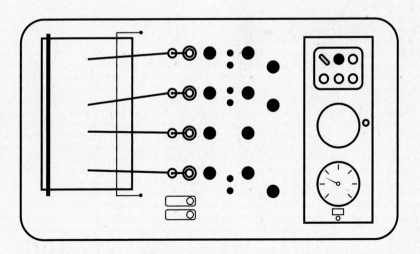

DON'T BE DOMINATED BY THE EXAMINER

The average polygraph test lasts about three hours. The longest part is the pretest interview, during which many people give away important information because they are off their guard. During this period, the examiner will try to convince you that the polygraph cannot be beaten and will try to induce feelings of guilt. Don't succumb to his tricks.

HOW TO FAKE YOUR RESPONSES

You need to ensure that the deviation from normal during your responses to control questions is greater than during the relevant questions. There are several ways to do this:

> **bite your tongue hard to trigger a pain response**
>
> **do math in your head, such as counting backwards in threes from a hundred**
>
> **think of something that makes you frightened**
>
> **alter your breathing rate**
>
> **tense your sphincter muscle**

NEVER MAKE A RELEVANT ADMISSION

This may seem obvious, but remember that the machine cannot detect lying, only your physiological responses, so don't admit to anything. The examiner can only work with what you tell him.

22. CHEAT A PARKING METER:

As everyone knows, a parking meter is a device used to collect money in exchange for the right to park a vehicle for a limited amount of time. Here are two ways of turning it into a device used to collect a small piece of cardboard or candy in exchange for parking for as long as you want. These methods won't work for the newer digital meters, but will save you a few quarters on the older types.

OUT OF ORDER

1. Park your car next to a meter with no time left on the clock.

2. Take a business card, matchbook, or any piece of semithick paper. Tear or cut a piece measuring 1.5 inches by 2.5 inches, then fold it twice lengthwise so that it measures about .25 inches by 2.5 inches and becomes quite rigid.

3. Stick the folded card into the quarter slot until you meet resistance and can't push it any further. When the card is about halfway into the slot, turn the handle on the meter all the way (you may have to use considerable force). This will draw the paper further into the slot. Keep turning the handle until the yellow "violation" sign appears. You have effectively jammed the machine into the "out-of-order" position. Don't turn the handle in the other direction or you'll make the red "ticket" sign appear and you'll have to drive away. As long as the yellow "violation" sign is showing, parking enforcement cannot ticket you, no matter how long you stay. On rare occasions, you may get chalked (the parking enforcer marks your tires with chalk and notes the time), which will give you about two hours of free parking, but most likely you can stay as long as you like.

Tear away any of the card that is still sticking out of the meter, otherwise the parking attendant may see it and pull it out. The next attendant that walks past will then issue you a ticket.

HAW FLAKES

Another way to beat the system is to purchase a packet of Haw Flakes: dark pink Chinese candy made from the fruit of the Chinese hawthorn, available in any Chinese food shop, or often given away as freebies when you visit a Chinese doctor. They come in rolls of twenty and cost about a nickel a roll. They are the same size as quarters, so if you stick them in the slot you're in business. Turn the handle gently, otherwise the candy will break.

23. COMMIT IDENTITY FRAUD:

Are your bills mounting up? Are bailiffs and loan sharks constantly knocking on your door? Maybe you just want to run up debts on someone else's credit cards.

IDENTITY CHANGE: PAPER TRIPPING

Although this method is not without its risks, it is the oldest system of identity change in existence. Simply wander around a large cemetery until you find the gravestone of a child who was born around the same time as you, but who died in infancy, without a Social Security number, bank account, or other forms of I.D. Make sure the child is of the same gender and race as you, then assume the identity of the dead infant. Use the information on the gravestone to obtain a copy of the birth certificate, which you can use to get other vital items of identification. State and local registrars are required by law to make birth and death records public, so you can easily access physical records at government offices.

The danger of this method is that there's no guarantee that the grave you choose hasn't already been visited by someone else with the same idea, often a member of the criminal fraternity. This means that your new identity could easily make you one of the FBI's ten most wanted.

IDENTITY FRAUD PHISHING SCAM

Send off thousands of emails at random saying that a major U.S. bank has gone bankrupt. On the email, include a link to an official-looking website that you have already set up. Your email advises that customers are starting to panic, so in response clients are advised to access their accounts to check that they are still in credit. Your website will contain a Trojan virus that captures user details for accessing their account, so that you can log in as them and steal money from their account. Launder the money by making false employment offers promising a significant income in a very short time, for allowing you to transfer a large sum into victim's accounts, which they must then transfer to (offshore) accounts that you have set up.

24. COUNTERFEIT MONEY:

You don't need anyone to point out the benefits of forging your own money over working in a soulless job for forty years. Before the arrival of desktop publishing, counterfeiting used to be an expensive operation, but now anyone can buy a PC, a scanner, and a high-end inkjet laser printer and become a paper millionaire without leaving their bedroom.

1. **Put a $50 bill on your scanner and scan it at the highest resolution (at least 2,400 dpi). The bill has several security features, some of which can be overcome with the scanner: the entire bill** is imprinted with a hexagonal pattern of faint and fine lines, as well as intricate etched details, all of which can be picked up in a high-resolution scan. The hard parts are finding the correct paper and the printing process. If you use a high-quality inkjet printer, the hexagons and intricate detailing will be preserved and will look convincing to the naked eye, even if they do not stand up to scrutiny under a magnifying glass.

2. Ordinary paper is made out of wood pulp. Counterfeit bills that have been printed on ordinary paper not only feel thicker and easily tear, they can be easily detected using a counterfeit pen which contains iodine (which changes color on contact with the cellulose in the paper). Real bills are printed on special "rag" paper that is made from cotton and linen fibers, which also contains minute red and blue silk threads. Obtain a supply of fine red and blue silk threads and mix them with a dilute non-water soluble adhesive, suspend them in water, and then spray the water evenly onto your rag paper. Press the sheets between Teflon rollers and allow to dry.

3. Some parts of the bill are printed in sparkly, color-shifting ink. Your printer won't be able to reproduce this, the plastic security strip, or the watermark. However, you could copy counterfeiter Ricky Scott Nelson, who took real $1 and $5 bills, masked the serial numbers, Treasury and Federal Reserve Seals, and the words "This note is legal tender." Then he bleached the bills and printed $50 and $100 detailing over the tops.

4. Print the fronts of several test bills, altering the hue, color balance, saturation, and contrast until you get the best color and definition match. Repeat with the back of the bill.

5. Print a double-sided bill, and keep only those where the front and back are perfectly aligned.

6. Spend small quantities of your fake cash in locations with low chances of detection (e.g., at nightclubs, where the light is poor, and staff may be too busy to check). For larger quantities, use them in drug transactions, sell them to foreign black marketers or drug dealers to use in scams, convert them to large denomination chips in Las Vegas, or take them to currency exchanges in Mexico.

25. CRACK A SAFE:

In the movies, safe cracking is as simple as performing a few twists and turns of a combination lock, while listening for the clicks with a stethoscope. With today's modern safes, this is still possible but very time consuming. However, every safe has a weakness, because it needs to be accessible to a locksmith if there is a malfunction or lock-out.

KNOW YOUR SAFE

Obtain blueprints of the safe so you know what obstacles you will face. There are two main types of safe: fire and burglary. The former has a thick layer of concrete and insulation to protect the contents from heat, while the latter has much greater protection against a break-in.

COMBINATION LOCKS

All safes are shipped from the manufacturer with try-out combinations (usually 100-50-100, or other industry standards widely known by locksmiths and safecrackers; these are available on the Internet, or from some of your criminal friends).

Try these first, because some idiots don't bother to change the combination; those who do, often use memorable numbers such as their date of birth, or they write it down somewhere (often near the safe, if not on the safe itself) because no one wants to be responsible for forgetting the number.

Many businesses keep their safes on day-lock, which either means that when the safe has been opened once during the day it remains unlocked, or only the last number of the combination is required to open it (easily found by trial and error).

Nobel Prize-winning physicist Richard Feynman discovered that the numbers do not need to be precise, and can be within a range, which greatly reduces the number of possible combinations. On the Internet, you can buy a motorized device that tries every combination in turn, but this takes time.

The counting-the-clicks method is very complicated and time consuming, and involves plotting your results on a graph (you don't see that in Oceans Eleven). To learn this technique read the classic book Techniques of Safecracking by Wayne B. Yeager.

DRILLING, TORCHING, AND BLASTING

Drill into the face of the lock to reach the lever or drive cam, then use a punch rod to push or bend the lever or drive cam out of the path of the bolt. Many safes now incorporate a cobalt plate to make drilling with anything less than a diamond-headed bit either impossible or incredibly slow. In some cases, you can drill diagonally, bypassing the cobalt plate, until you reach the wheel pack of the combination lock. Then use a small fiber-optic viewer called a borescope to watch how the wheels are turning.

Often drilling isn't an option because the safe has a further level of protection called a relocker, which triggers extra locking devices when a drill passes through a piece of glass or plastic inside the safe's walls. If this happens, you'll need some explosives or cutters.

Oxy-acetylene torches reach temperatures of 4500°F and will burn a hole in the safe wall, unless it is fitted with extra protection (such as copper plates that conduct heat away from the site). For this reason, plasma cutters are more popular. It gets the gas so hot that the atoms begin to split, generating very high temperatures.

If time is short, use what is known in the trade as a "jam shot" to blow off the doors using a few ounces of nitroglycerin (also known as "grease," it is a mixture of glycerin, nitric acid, and sulfuric acid) or C-4 (plastic explosive) placed in the space between the safe door and the frame.

26. CREATE CROP CIRCLES:

According to some New Age groups, crop circles are messages from aliens or are extraterrestrial landing sites made by "tachyonic energy," a sort of weird cosmic vibe that creates and maintains order in the chaos of matter. However, the sane among us know that they are created by a group of (often inebriated) friends armed only with rope and some planks of wood.

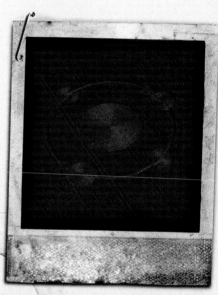

WHERE DID CROP CIRCLES BEGIN?

Two British artists, Doug Bower and Dave Chorley started the craze. One summer evening in 1978 after a few pints at the bar, they made their first crop circle on their hands and knees with a four-foot metal bar. Their efforts were rewarded with worldwide interest, and they continued to make crop circles for over a decade.

HOW TO MAKE AN ALIEN LANDING STRIP

1. Choose your location carefully. The best place is a sloped field that can be seen from a road, so that a

maximum number of passers-by can be freaked out by its
unique and mysterious beauty.

2. Use a PC and spend a long time planning your design
and its execution, so that when you get in the field you
won't be faced with an impossible task. A basic design
should incorporate an arrangement of discs in a geometric
formation. Gather a team of like-minded hoaxers from
your local drinking establishment, and give everyone a
designated area to work on.

3. Make your crop circle under cover of night during
dry conditions, and access the field using an existing
farm track. Your basic tool is a piece of wood with a hole
drilled at each end, and a rope attached through the holes.
Hold the rope loop while you flatten the corn forward and
down, keeping one foot on the wooden bar.

4. To make a circle, one person stands in the center
holding one end of the rope; a second person holds the
other end of the rope to form the radius of the circle,
and walks around the first person, flattening the corn to
create the circumference. Then the wooden plank tool can
be used to flatten the area inside the circle. You can also
use a small lawn roller, available at most garden centers.
To make more complex shapes, make construction lines by
laying rope outlines.

5. When you've finished, add some extraterrestrial
details such as melted iron filings which make convincing
"meteorite particles," or scatter around some disemboweled
cows. Complete your design just before dawn, then you
can take a photo of it before all the "croppies" arrive.
Make sure you remove all evidence of human involvement,
including cigarette butts (assuming you are stupid enough
to smoke around dry corn) and empty beer cans.

27. MAKE MOONSHINE:

Moonshine, popskull, stumphole, ruckus juice, hillbilly pop, happy Sally: whatever you want to call it, making illegal alcohol is still one of the most enjoyable ways of breaking the law, evading federal taxes, and losing your eyesight. It takes lots of time and practice before you can whip up an impurity-free batch that won't do you serious damage. Use it in your lawnmower until you are confident enough to open a speakeasy.

SPROUT THE CORN

"Sprout" five pounds of shelled whole corn to convert the cornstarch into sugar. Put the corn into a container with a slow-drainage hole, cover with warm water, drape a cloth over the mouth, and leave it for three days (or until the sprouts are about two inches long), adding more warm water as required. Dry the sprouts and grind them to make cornmeal (alternatively, buy five pounds of cornmeal and skip this step).

MASH

Make a "mash" by adding twenty gallons of boiling water and twenty pounds of sugar to the cornmeal. When the mash has cooled to "warm" add one and a half ounces of yeast. Leave in a warm place for about three days to ferment (or until the mash stops bubbling). Now the mash has been converted to carbonic acid and alcohol and is called "sour mash."

DISTILLATION

Distill the mash by heating it to 173°F in a copper moonshine still. At this temperature, the alcohol (ethanol) rises to the top of the still, and then travels along to the cooling part of the still, where it condenses again and can be collected. It will be a clear liquid the color of dark beer.

SINGLINGS

The first liquid to condense from the still contains volatile oils, and should be discarded. After that, the liquid can be collected into glass jars called "singlings." The liquid collected at the end of the run is called "low wine" and is only about 10 percent proof, so it can be added to the mash barrel and distilled again. Stop distilling once a tablespoon of low wine thrown on a naked flame refuses to burn.

DISTILL AGAIN, AND AGAIN

Empty the mash (it can be added to the next batch of grain). The ethanol collected in the first singlings will have the highest proof, and the proof level drops as the process continues. However, all the singlings will need to be distilled one or two more times to remove impurities. After three distillations, some of your singlings will contain ethanol up to 150 proof (that's about 75 percent alcohol).

28. TEN THINGS YOU SHOULDN'T SAY TO A COP:

When you get pulled over by the cops, there's a right way and a wrong way to handle the situation. Here are some wiseass comments that are guaranteed to get you arrested.

1. Can't we all get along? Well then, go ahead and beat me up: I need the money to start my own rap label.

2. Why don't we discuss this over a box of donuts?

3. I pay your salary and for the freeway, so I'll speed if I want to, damn it.

4. I wasn't going as fast as that guy in front. Yeah, you can't see him any more because he's so far ahead.

5. What do you mean, "Have I been drinking?" You don't think I drive that fast and talk this slow when I'm sober, do you?

6. Don't bother to taser me. I already have a hard-on, see?

7. Is it true that people become cops because they are too dumb to work at McDonalds?

8. I'll show you my license if you show me your boobs.

9. Well, when I reached down to pick up my bag of crack, my gun fell off my lap and got lodged between the brake pedal and the gas pedal, forcing me to speed out of control.

10. Aren't you the guy from the Village People?

29. PULL A PRACTICAL JOKE IN THE TOILET:

If you would rather feed your toes to a moray eel than conduct yourself with dignity and discretion in the bathroom, here are a few ideas to bring a little bit of excitement to an otherwise ordinary day.

1. In 1933, Ralph Wiley, a Dow Chemical lab worker, accidentally discovered polyvinylidene chloride, or Saran wrap. After World War II, this material was approved for food packaging, but the first occasion it was stretched across the top of a toilet bowl resulting in maximum splashback for an unsuspecting victim has been lost to time. However, it remains one of the simplest fraternity-style toilet pranks in the world. Wrap under the seat and do not leave any give-away creases.

2. In a public toilet, turn the nozzles of the hand dryers upside down and fill them with flour or talcum powder.

When they are switched on, they will shower the room with fluffy white clouds.

3. Smear Vaseline, peanut butter, a melted chocolate bar, or any industrial lubricant on the faucet and toilet handles.

4. In a restroom with sensor toilets, place duct tape over the sensor so that it never flushes, or tape over the faucet sensor so the water stays on.

5. Remove the toilet tank lid and look inside. Locate a little horizontal plastic tube about a quarter-inch in diameter. Turn it outwards and point it towards the front of the tank, so that when you put the lid back the end is poking out but hidden by the lip of the lid. When your victim flushes, they will get soaked by a spurt of water.

6. Leave a water balloon or packet of ketchup under the toilet seat. When your victim sits down they will get soaked by a miniexplosion.

7. Add five packets of gelatin mix to the toilet bowl and wait a few hours for it to solidify. This results in an uncomfortable and embarrassing splashback every time.

8. The Chinese Fire Drill is another classic dorm bathroom prank. Everyone fills a bucket with water. Set a paper bag on fire and throw it under the stall door while your victim is taking a dump. Then yell "Fire" as everyone throws their bucketful of water over the top of the stall.

30. TEN GRAFFITI TIPS:

Why say it when you can spray it? Whether you are doing a tag (stylized signature), piece (a large 3D image), throwie (somewhere between a tag and a piece), dub (two-color piece), burner (a large elaborate piece), or a back-to-back (graffiti that covers a wall or train from end to end), here are some dope graffiti tips.

1. Develop a kick ass tag by writing your name over and over until you know it looks good. Come up with a writing style, and practice. . . . Practice is everything.

2. Only "go over" someone else's work if you want to diss them and declare war. Most writers respect other writer's pieces, except newbies ("toys") who are whack. It's OK to paint over a piece if it has already been slashed, or if you can create something better (i.e., you can "burn" the other writer).

3. Increase your credibility by painting "heavens" in hard-to-reach places such as rooftops—which will make your piece hard to remove and long lasting. The remotest spots are usually the most dangerous.

4. Can control is the basis of all graff work. If you can't learn how to spray thick and thin lines (pull back), and fill without causing blobs and drips, stay off the street. Before you start spraying, hold the can upside down and let out a few seconds of spray air (pressure), then shake the can hard for about thirty seconds. Then you should be able to spray with less mist and drips and you'll stand more chance of busting a clean piece.

5. It's OK to use cheap paint to tag, but steal some quality paint for bigger pieces. However, your skill is always more important that your tools. Toys always blame their cheap cans.

6. Think BIG and use bold colors. That doesn't mean you have to use real colors. For example, hair can be blue or purple. It doesn't have to be black or yellow. Always think style, style, style. You've got to develop your own style.

7. If you're into markers, get some Sharpie Magnums. They're industrial strength, dry quickly, and mark on wet and oily surfaces. They're huge and cost less than five bucks.

8. Every graffiti artist has a "black book" which they use to jot down and try out ideas. Get one, use it.

9. To do big, complex pieces, join a crew. You'll already have produced stylish pieces that show off your unique style. The crew will be headed by a king or queen who will be the best artist among its members.

31. WALK ON HOT COALS:

Common sense says that mind over matter just doesn't figure when it comes to flame grilling your feet. After all, when you toss a steak on the barbecue, it cooks regardless of whatever positive thoughts it is entertaining. Fire walking boils down to thermal conductivity and how you rake the coals; it has little to do with how you walk or what you're thinking, so this explanation is more of a "why it works" than a "how-to."

LEIDENFROST EFFECT

This is named for Johann Gottlob Leidenfrost, who described the effect in his manuscript *A Tract About Some Qualities of Common Water* (1756). The Leidenfrost effect makes it possible for a person to plunge their wet hand briefly into a vat of molten lead without injury, to blow liquid nitrogen from their mouth, and many believe, to fire walk. Leidenfrost discovered that when a liquid comes into contact with a mass that is much hotter than the liquid's boiling point, instead of evaporating quickly, a thin layer of vapor forms between the liquid and the hot mass which acts as an insulator, increasing the time it takes to boil. Although there is disagreement about whether this applies to walking on hot coals, those who believe that the Leidenfrost effect comes into play here argue that sweat and normal body moisture on the soles of the feet turn to vapor and protect them from the high temperatures of the coals. Also, many fire walks take place on grass, so it is easy for the feet to pick up further moisture, especially if the grass is wet.

POOR CONDUCTION

The most significant factor is the heat of the coals versus their ability to conduct that heat. Just because a material is red hot does not make it dangerous. For example, the heat shield tiles on the Space Shuttle are such poor conductors of thermal energy that you can handle them while they are glowing. Coals burn at approximately 600°C, but the surface heat will be absorbed by your feet, especially if the embers are wood, which is a poor conductor. If the coals were replaced with hot metal (an excellent conductor) you could kiss your feet goodbye. (Remember your piece of steak? That cooks on the barbecue because it is sitting on a griddle made of metal.) Also, the coals cool quickly when they are raked out over a wide area.

In short, so long as you keep up a steady pace, you can use the mantra "hot coals, hot coals, third degree burns" while you are walking, and you still won't get so much as a blister.

32. BE EXCUSED FROM JURY DUTY:

Jury duty is an important and much appreciated duty, but unless you're given a big case like O.J. or Michael Jackson, you can't make any money selling your story afterwards, so you need to know how to qualify for an exemption. Inconvenience or work commitments are not accepted reasons to be excused. But there are plenty of other ways to beat the draft.

Requests to be excused will not be accepted by phone. If after reading the advice below you think you qualify for an exemption, submit your request in writing on your jury summons, answering each question under penalty of perjury (that means don't get caught lying).

1. You cannot be a juror if you are a convicted felon. So steal a car and then turn yourself in to the cops. If they let you off with a caution, call the officer a pussy and break his nose with your forehead. That will get you out of jury duty for life.

2. Permanent disabilities and mental health issues will also exempt you. When the jury summons arrives, cut off a finger with a chain saw or fake an overdose, but make sure someone finds you before you bleed to death or slip into a coma. If you are requesting to be excused for medical reasons, you must also include a letter from your doctor.

3. Buy a small field and plant some corn. In some states, self-employed people or those who are paid by 100 percent commission are exempt, as are farmers during planting or harvesting season.

4. People over sixty-five years of age can be excused if they desire.

5. Students and stay-at-home mothers of small children may be temporarily excused. So get pregnant or go back to school.

6. Get your five year old to scribble on the jury summons "i can not reed or rite" or "No comprende" (jurors must be able to read, write, and understand English).

33. ELEVATOR HACKS:

You don't have to be a claustrophobic sociopath to hate elevators. The worst thing about them is what also makes public transport suck: you have to keep stopping to let other people get on. If you refuse to surrender control of your life, here are a few ways to get the most out of your next elevator ride.

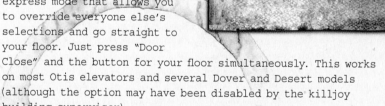

EXPRESS SERVICE

Lots of elevators have an express mode that allows you to override everyone else's selections and go straight to your floor. Just press "Door Close" and the button for your floor simultaneously. This works on most Otis elevators and several Dover and Desert models (although the option may have been disabled by the killjoy building supervisor).

WHEN YOU PRESS THE WRONG BUTTON

Some elevators have "static sensitive" buttons—you just have to run your finger over them to light them up. When you press the wrong button (or several are lit up by people waiting on those floors), override the system by lighting up the whole bank of numbers by brushing over them with your sleeve. The computer will reset itself by putting out all the lights. Then just touch the floor you want and go straight there without an interruption.

In many push button lifts, if you hit the wrong button you can simply press it again and keep holding it down. This triggers the elevator's "stuck button protection" feature, which is designed to ensure that it won't stay at a particular floor if a button becomes stuck.

EMERGENCY STOP

Try this if you don't mind being stuck between floors for a couple hours until rescuers arrive. When you jump up and down inside a moving elevator with sufficient force, sensors detect the jerks caused by your irrepressible exuberance and disregard for your own safety. The elevator will decide the rope has snapped and engage the brakes. Look up and watch as your small intestine smacks against the ceiling.

34. FIVE WAYS TO KILL YOUR PC:

If your PC crashes at random intervals, you can germinate seeds while it boots up, or it is so old that you wish it would just die so you can move on with your life, here are some ways to hasten its demise.

Don't be sentimental. Sure, you have enjoyed some epic multiplayer online gaming sessions together, and its hard drive has seen more hard-core pornography come and go than Hugh Hefner's closet. But some PCs are prime candidates for assisted suicide.

1. Power supplies account for about 30 percent of all dead-PC occurrences. Their job is to filter 240 volts down to bite-sized 12V, 5V, and 3.3V DC allocations that modern PCs need. So if you want to screw up your PC, buy a cheap power supply and don't use a surge protector (or just stick a chisel into it). With luck, you'll scorch some of the motherboard and toast the RAM. Alternatively, flick the little red self-destruct switch on the power supply: the one that changes between 115 and 230 volts.

2. Keep your PC on the floor and let it accumulate dust. Never vacuum on or near it. Eventually the cooling fan will get clogged up and your ICU will overheat. If you can't wait that long, just unplug the fan or remove the heatsink and the processor will cook itself to death in a matter of seconds.

3. Loosen some of the components, such as the RAM, so that it is seated incorrectly. When you boot up, it will short out and, ideally, melt the slot as well, filling the room with the smell of singed hair.

4. During a lightening storm, leave your PC plugged into the power supply, and the modem plugged into the wall. Hopefully, your house will get struck by lightning, frying not only your PC, but any other piece of electrical equipment that is plugged into the mains. Static electricity is also a PC killer. Rub your feet back and forth on a synthetic carpet while wearing shoes, then touch your mouse; you should get enough static electricity that shocks you and fries the mouse and keyboard. Open up the PC case and you can destroy computer components just by touching them, thanks to electrostatic discharge (ESD).

6. Overclocking is the act of increasing the speed of certain components in a computer beyond what is specified by the manufacturer. In some BIOS's you can alter your CPU speed and fry your computer without even taking the back off. When you boot your PC, enter your BIOS (usually by pressing Del, F1, or F10) then change your CPU speed or voltage to the highest number. Then sit back and wait for the sparks.

35. BECOME A RELIGIOUS ICON:

Long before you start building your fan base and drawing really big crowds, you need to ask yourself some tough questions. Being a Messiah isn't just about riding donkeys and performing miracles (though this will take up a lot of your time). It's a major lifestyle choice where every aspect of your personality will be brought into the public domain and placed under intense scrutiny. Plus, it's a highly competitive area, with new Messiahs ready to step into your sandals immediately after your inevitable crucifixion.

YOUR IMAGE

Lose weight. Messiahs tend to be average to underweight. Accentuate with baggy clothing.

Wear comfortable shoes and grow a beard. Sadly, this rules out most women under the age of fifty, making the job of Messiah a very male-biased arena.

Put whitener on your teeth. Messiahs always have bright teeth.

Try to cut down on any bad habits like swearing, picking your nose, smoking, and having casual sex. You'll soon be dying for the sins of the world and you don't want to lessen the impact of your self-sacrifice by getting lung cancer or AIDS.

CREATE A BUZZ

Relocate to a hot and dry country. For some reason Messiahs never really take off in places where average rainfall exceeds twenty inches per year.

The best way to build your status as Messiah is to deliberately shun publicity by avoiding large crowds. Take every opportunity to go fishing with a few close friends. Frequently lock yourself in the toilet and say you need time alone to think, or better still, wander off into the desert for a few weeks. (Make sure your agent knows where you are.) This introspective and enigmatic behavior will soon lead to a booking on the Late Show with David Letterman.

Call everyone "my child" but don't be patronizing. People hate that. Also, touch everyone you meet on the top of the head.

Start hanging out with prostitutes, the poor, the sick, and the unemployed. Not only will this make you appear compassionate, but after your death, it will be the money and blind hope of these unhappy, gullible, and disenfranchised folk that will quickly turn you into a global phenomenon.

BE VAGUE

If anyone asks you whether you are the Messiah, deny it (even if you really are). Then lock yourself in the toilet.

Tell everyone how great your dad's house is. They will assume you are talking about Heaven (don't mention that he lives in a motel in Detroit).

Use lots of metaphors when speaking to the crowds that inevitably form whenever you leave the house. Talk inaudibly. This will create an atmosphere of awed silence in your presence, while also making you appear humble. Popular topics of conversation include bread and sheep.

PERFORM MIRACLES

Do not attempt any "magic" tricks—everyone hates magicians. Stick to the basic repertoire of killing shrubs, healing the sick, and raising the dead.

CRUCIFIXION

Just before your death it is good practice to throw a quiet dinner party for twelve of your closest friends. Make an effort—don't just offer them bread and wine—you'll look like a cheapskate. Also, don't freak them out by saying stuff like "Eat me" or they'll be reaching for their coats before you can say "transubstantiation."

RESURRECTION

Arrange for a friend to break into the mortuary after your death and steal your body.

36. MAKE A COURT APPEARANCE:

You don't get a second chance to make a first impression and this is never truer than when you make a court appearance. Here are some things you need to think about to prepare.

BE SMART

Your appearance is vitally important. If you aren't wearing an orange prison suit, dress neatly in clean clothes and ask your witnesses and supporters to do the same. Remove your hat and any visible piercings before entering the courtroom. Don't put anything shiny or greasy in your hair such as wet-look gel. Keep jewelry to a minimum: in the eyes of the court, bling alone is a good enough reason to keep you off the streets. Do not attend court under the influence of drugs or alcohol, and do not eat, drink, smoke, or chew gum in the courtroom.

BE PUNCTUAL

Go to the courtroom and check in with the clerk, then stay there until your name and case are called. Arrive on time, and, if possible, arrive early to allow time to compose yourself. If you arrive rushed, you will take that tension into the courtroom and it will harm your credibility. Missing a hearing altogether may result in a contempt of court charge against you.

BE ARTICULATE

When you are addressed by the judge you should stand, then speak politely, clearly, and calmly using good language (do not swear or use slang, unless you are quoting what someone said). Address the judge as "Your honor." Speak only to the judge and attorneys; do not address other witnesses or the jury directly.

STAY CALM

Don't interrupt the attorney or the judge, and don't argue with them. The judge's word is final. If you refuse to obey him/her, you may be held in contempt of court. The best way to lose a case is to lose your temper. Stay calm. We've all seen witnesses and defendants losing it in courtroom dramas on TV, and their outburst is nearly always followed by a smug-looking attorney saying "No further questions, your honor" and returning to his seat in triumph. The opposing attorney will try to attack your credibility and get you to argue with him/her so you lose your composure. Don't fall for it.

37. LIGHT A FART ON FIRE:

Do you really think there's more to lighting your farts than holding a naked flame next to your butt while you break wind? Well there isn't. A search for "fart light" on You Tube will return over 400 examples of guys with no prior training doing just that. However, here are three ways NOT to ignite an air biscuit:

Don't attempt to cut the cheese near a naked flame when you need to use the toilet, otherwise there's an increased risk of follow through. Here's an extreme example of what we mean:

www.metacafe.com/watch/313171/
how _ not _ to _ light _ a _ fart/

Do not use any artificial combustants such as deodorant aerosols:

www.metacafe.com/watch/305430/
fire _ in _ the _ hole _ 2/

Finally, don't attempt to ignite your flatus in company if you can't produce any gas. Because you're then you're going to look really dumb:

www.youtube.com/watch?v=F1PgIQU2yq8

After all, if you can't even manage to light a fart, what the hell can you do, dumb-ass?

38. OBSCURE WAYS TO GET ARRESTED IN 25 STATES:

In Alabama, you can be arrested for operating a vehicle blindfolded, wearing a fake moustache that causes laughter in church, flicking boogers in the wind, or keeping an ice cream in your back pocket.

Alaskans are forbidden from pushing a live moose from an airplane, waking a bear to take a picture, or taking a kangaroo (even willingly) into a barber shop.

In Arizona, it is illegal to hunt camels, and a driver who removes or ignores barricades at a flooded wash faces a minimum $2,000 fine.

In Arkansas, it is illegal to mispronounce Arkansas.

In California, it is against the law for anyone to stop a child from jumping over puddles of water, and a city ordinance states anyone who detonates a nuclear device within city limits will be fined $500.

In Colorado, a woman can only wear a red dress on the streets before 7 P.M. Also, you can't drive a black car on Sunday in Denver.

You will break the law in Connecticut when your bicycle reaches speeds in excess of 65 mph or when you walk across the street on your hands.

In Delaware, "R" rated movies cannot be shown at drive-in theaters, and it is illegal to fly over any body of water without adequate provision of food and drink.

Florida women can be fined for falling asleep under a hair dryer, and in Miami it is illegal for anyone to imitate an animal. Sex with a porcupine (unless you are a porcupine) is also prohibited; in fact any form of sexual contact other than missionary position is a misdemeanor.

You can't tie a giraffe to a lamppost in Georgia, or keep your donkey in the bathtub. As if that wasn't bad enough, all sex toys are banned.

In Hawaii, you can be fined for not owning a boat or for sticking coins in your ears.

In Idaho, you can't ride a merry-go-round on a Sunday, or fish on a camel's back under any circumstances.

Illinois law expressly forbids giving lighted cigars to dogs, cats, and other domesticated pets. Eating in a restaurant that is on fire, peeing in your neighbor's mouth, and drinking beer out of a bucket while sitting on the curb are all off limits.

Indiana disallows bathing during the winter, or attending a cinema or theater or riding a public streetcar within four hours after eating garlic. All hotel sheets must be exactly ninety-nine inches long and eighty-one inches wide.

In Iowa, kisses may not last longer than five minutes, and a man with a moustache may not kiss a woman in public. Horses are forbidden to eat fire hydrants.

Kansas condemns the use of ice cream on cherry pie, whale hunting, snowball fights, and screaming at haunted houses.

A woman in Kentucky must get her husband's permission before buying a hat, and anyone who has been drinking is "sober" until he or she "cannot hold onto the ground."

In Louisiana, biting someone with your natural teeth is "simple assault," but if you have false teeth you will be charged with "aggravated assault." Having a pizza delivered to someone without their permission will land you with a $500 fine.

Maine prohibits leaving an airplane during a flight, leaving your Christmas decorations up too long, or walking down the street with your shoelaces untied.

You cannot swear while inside the city limits of Baltimore, Maryland; give or receive oral sex anywhere; or allow thistles to grow in your yard.

In Massachusetts, you are breaking the law if you get a tattoo or body piercing, eat more than three sandwiches at a wake, take a dump on your neighbor, or wear a goatee beard without paying for a license.

When in Michigan, you are prevented from using a decompression chamber to kill your dog, swearing in front of your wife and children, or letting your pig run free in Detroit unless it has a ring in its nose.

Minnesota law prohibits walking across the Minnesota-Wisconsin border with a duck on your head; giving or receiving oral sex; or having sex with your wife if your breath stinks of garlic, onions, or sardines.

In Mississippi, it is illegal to teach others the meaning of polygamy, to parent more than one illegitimate child, or to seduce a woman with a false promise of marriage.

The law in Missouri precludes the installation of bathtubs with four legs resembling animal paws in Kansas City, or the rescuing of women who are in their nightgowns by firemen in St. Louis.

39. VENDING MACHINES AND THEIR WEAKNESSES:

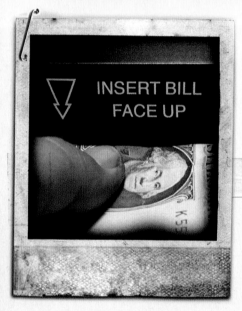

INSERT BILL
FACE UP

All vending machines have weaknesses or special codes contained in their programming that allow the vending machine engineers to open them up, diagnose problems, and get them to deliver free soda and snacks faster than the Japanese can make Toyotas.

COCA-COLA HACK

This hack only seems to work on Coca-Cola machines. It fools the machine into thinking it has taken your dollar bill, then you pull it back out again. Take a crisp dollar bill and lay it with George Washington face up and looking left. Put some Scotch tape along the white edge of the bill closest to you, turn over, and repeat. Then add more layers to make a handle, so that when the bill goes into the machine you can hold onto the tape until the validator clicks, which is your sign to pull the bill out again.

PEPSI HACK

Find a Pepsi machine with an LED screen. Enter the engineer's access code by using the keypad or drink selection buttons (where button 1 is the top, and 2 is the next one down; or where the buttons are side by side, 1 is the far left, 2 is the next one to the right, and so on). Punch in 1, 3, 2, 4. This is the default access sequence, which can be changed to another combination, but rarely is. This should get you into the machine's menu, from which you can play around to find the free drink option.

SNACK HACK

Insert coins and make your selection, but hold the release flap up on the bottom so the machine thinks it didn't drop your food. Then press the coin return button to get your money back.

40. PRANK PHONE CALLS:

There's a thin line between humor and harassment, but so long as you don't threaten the other person or keep phoning them over and over, you won't have much to worry about. Here are ten good prank ideas, and some of them don't even rely on the receiver having a limited IQ or a high gullibility quotient.

1. Call a shopping mall or bar and ask them to put out a call for any one of these missing persons: Mike Hunt, Connie Lingus, Holden McGroin, Clint Torres, Hal Djakok, Hugh Douche, Jim Nasium, Mike Ockhertz, Phil Miaz, Oliver Clothesoff, Mike Rotch, or Maya Buttreeks.

2. Phone an Internet provider and explain politely that you surf the net for porn for at least eight hours each day and that you are phoning to inquire whether they can provide you with a cybersex package.

3. Call up someone's cell and tell them you are from their mobile provider and that their cell phone number was

recently auctioned off. In order to continue with their cell phone service, they need to come in to the shop to get a new SIM card.

4. Pretend to be from a local photo developer, and explain that you have some of their photos that haven't been picked up yet. However, point out that there is a problem: some of the photos were of explicit content and couldn't be developed.

5. Call up an Alzheimers 800 number help line and tell them you need help, but can't remember your name or where you live.

6. Phone a carpet cleaning company and ask them how to get blood and urine out of your carpet.

7. Pretend you're an assassin and that you've been hired by the person you are calling, but you need them to tell you the name and address of the hit. When the conversation gets hairy, tell them to stay put and you'll come over to sort out the details in person.

8. Find out some interesting stuff about a complete stranger. Pretend to be conducting a survey for a leading woman's magazine (it can be about food, sex, pets, whatever). Have a load of questions already prepared. Start off with some harmless questions to put the other person at ease, then make them increasingly bizarre.

9. Pretend to be the FBI calling to alert them to the fact that you are aware that they have been accessing illegal porn sites on the Internet. Explain that this is a warning, and that if you continue they will be arrested. If you're lucky enough to have picked a pervert, this should really freak them out.

10. Phone up a televangelist and tell them that ever since you've watched their show you are convinced that you are Jesus Christ. Thank him for making you realize your true calling.

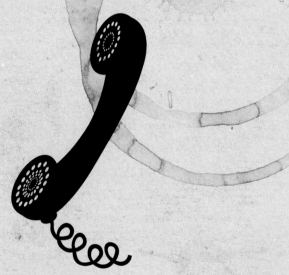

41. TEN BACHELOR PARTY IDEAS:

Bachelor parties are all about guys hooking up to get loud and stupid, all in the name of male bonding. Here are nine ideas for an occasion to remember.

1. Call the local undertakers and report the bachelor dead. Arrange to have his corpse picked up at his house on the day of the bachelor party when he's at home.

2. Paste a fake skipper's beard on the bachelor's chin and tell him that he can be the skipper of a sixty-foot yacht for the day (which you've rented). After a great time on the waves, with good food and plenty of fishing, finish the trip with a skinny dip off the side of the boat. Only then will the bachelor realize that all his friends have shaved off their pubes.

3. Stripping down the bachelor's Chevy and reassembling it in his bedroom is good; demolishing his house and stuffing the pieces into his car is even better.

4. If you're driving home at the end of the night and the bachelor falls asleep, get everyone else in the car to scream at the same time like you're about to crash.

5. Get six cans of beer, and shake one of them hard, then play German Roulette: mix up the cans so no one knows which one will go off. Take turns putting a can to your head and risk getting wasted.

6. For a whole hour everyone has to take a mouthful of beer every minute. Anyone who needs to take a leak has to down their pint first. Then everyone takes a trip to the ER to get their stomachs pumped.

7. Get the bachelor to drink a gallon of milk and try to keep it down. There's no way he'll manage it, and he'll be projectile vomiting within half an hour.

8. For a cheap night out, if the bachelor is diabetic, dissolve a whole bag of sugar in his beer. He'll wake up in the ER a week later with the worst hangover/near-death-experience of his life.

9. Plant some Class A drugs on the bachelor. Then the best man, who is driving, gets the car pulled over by the cops for speeding. The bachelor gets tasered, spends a night getting buggered in a cell, his wife-to-be has to post bail, and he gets a criminal record (making his law degree a waste of three years, and if he's already done time, he could go down for life).

42. TEN BACHELORETTE PARTY IDEAS:

Bachelorette parties are the ideal time to let your hair down, get hammered, and objectify men, all in the name of female bonding. Here are ten ideas for a night to remember.

1. Learn how to strip. Arrange a class by getting a professional stripper or lap dancer to come to your house and teach you and your girlfriends.

2. Take turns putting a condom on a cucumber or banana with your mouth. Award points for speed, style, and dirtiness.

3. On your night out, see who can collect the most pairs of men's briefs. Award points for skidmarks and other stains.

4. Make it a rule that girls can only use their left hand for drinking (except those who are left-handed). If anyone forgets and breaks the rule, a loud chant of "bamma" goes up and continues until she has downed her drink.

5. Make the bachelorette get a foot massage from a stranger.

6. Give everyone a bingo card with photos, drawings, or descriptions of different types of men (e.g., fat bastard, poseur, granddad, jail bait, etc.). The first woman who gets a kiss from one of each type from her card is the winner.

8. Get the bride's father to dress up as a fireman (with a very dark visor) and be the stripper.

9. See how many men with the same name as the groom the bachelorette can make out with.

10. Have a passion party, where you hire a passion consultant to show you a range of adult toys and sex aids.

43. OBSCURE WAYS TO GET ARRESTED IN ANOTHER 25 STATES:

Montana prohibits married women from going fishing alone on Sundays, and unmarried women from fishing alone at all.

If your child burps in church in Nebraska you can be arrested, and you need a state license to give your daughter a perm.

In Nevada, if you shoot some-one's dog on their property, the law allows them to hang you.

New Hampshire law forbids tapping of feet, head nod-ding, and all other ways of keeping time to music in a tavern, restaurant, or cafe. Picking seaweed from the beach is also illegal.

When committing a murder in New Jersey, it is illegal to wear a bullet-proof vest. You're not allowed to pump your own gas, and in Newark it is illegal to buy ice cream after 6:00 P.M.

Women are strictly forbidden to appear unshaven in public in New Mexico, and you cannot own an unexpurgated version of Romeo and Juliet, or dance around a sombrero.

In New York, you can be fined $25 for flirting. The second time you appear before a court for looking at women in a lewd way, you may be forced to wear horse blinders, and you'll get the death penalty for jumping from a skyscraper.

Possession of a lottery ticket in North Carolina may result in a $2,000 fine. Singing off key, indulging in oral sex, and serving alcohol at a bingo game are all illegal.

North Dakota bans sleeping with your shoes on, the serving of beer and pretzels at the same time in a bar or restaurant, and women wearing open-toed footwear.

You can get arrested in Ohio for getting a fish drunk, or sharing a house with more than four other women (if you're a woman). In Oxford, it's illegal for a woman to strip off her clothing while standing in front of a man's picture.

Oklahoma condemns bar owners who allow their customers to simulate sex with a buffalo. The state also prohibits making ugly faces at a dog or taking a bite from someone else's hamburger.

Oregon eschews the carrying of babies on the running board of a vehicle, talking dirty during sex, and using canned corn as fishing bait.

In Pennsylvania, you cannot sleep on top of a refrigerator outdoors, sing in the bathtub, or catch a fish with your hands.

When in Rhode Island, refrain from coasting downhill in your car with your transmission in neutral. On a Sunday in Providence, it is illegal for shop owners to sell toothpaste and toothbrushes to the same customer.

In South Carolina, the only time and place you can beat your wife is Sunday morning on the steps of the state house. Tattoos are as illegal as keeping your horse in the bathtub.

In South Dakota, lying down and falling asleep in a cheese factory is actionable behavior, and movies that show cops being beaten up are banned.

Tennessee considers it a felony to sell hollow logs, drive while asleep, or eat roadkill.

You can't sell an eye in Texas, nor should you take more than three sips of beer at a time while standing, or milk another person's cow.

In Utah, you are breaking the law if you persistently tread on the cracks between paving stones on the sidewalk of a state highway. You cannot have sex in the back of an ambulance while it is responding to an emergency call.

In Vermont, they'll throw the book at you (but not the Good Book) for denying the existence of God.

Driving without shoes is illegal in Virginia, as is trick-or-treating on Halloween, tickling women, and hunting on Sunday (except raccoons which may be slaughtered until 2:00 A.M.).

In Washington, you would be ill-advised to suck a lolli-pop or pretend your parents are rich. If you are a motorist with criminal intentions, you are advised to stop at the city limits and telephone the chief of police before entering.

In West Virginia, a man can have sex with an animal as long as the animal does not exceed forty pounds.

Wisconsin does not tolerate the serving of butter substi-tutes in state prisons, kissing on a train, or making cheese without a license.

Three ways to get arrested in Wyoming are being drunk in a mine, wearing a hat in a theater that obstructs other people's views, or taking a picture of a rabbit from January to April without an official permit.

44. SLOT MACHINE TIPS:

Slot machines are designed to take in more money than they pay out. Everyone knows that. However, what you probably don't know is that in a casino, not all the machines are set to pay out the same percentage of what they take, which can be anywhere from 90 to 98 percent. The art of improving your odds of winning are to locate the "loose" machines and ignore the "tight" ones.

LOOSE VS. TIGHT

A machine that is set to pay out a high percentage of what it takes in (as much as 98 percent) is "loose," and a machine that pays out less (as low as 90 percent) is "tight."

The higher the stake, the higher the percentage payout. The $5 or higher machines are set to pay out the highest percentage of what they take, while the quarter and nickel machines pay out the lowest percentage.

LOCATE THE LOOSE SLOTS

Loose slots are used to encourage other players to keep spending their money. When players win money, casinos want them to be visible, so loose slots are frequently situated near change booths; on elevated carousels; near coffee shops, cafes, and snack bars (to make people eat quickly and get back to spending money); and on "crosswalks" which are places players must walk through to reach other slot aisles.

AVOID THE TIGHT SLOTS

Tight slots can be found tucked away in places where there aren't many passers-by. Loose slots used to be placed near casino entrances, so that the sound of people winning would entice other players in. However, this strategy soon backfired, as people stayed at the entrance, winning and not venturing further. Now the slots at entrances are tight to medium.

Tight machines are also placed near sportsbook/racing areas and gaming tables, because people who bet on that kind of action do not want to be distracted by hearing large jackpots being paid out on the nearby slots. Besides, these gamblers spend more money where they are, so casinos want them to stay put. Near ticket and show lines you will find more tight slots, because people there have stopped gambling and are unlikely to leave the line to play the slots again if they hear someone win.

Slots outside restrooms are always tight, because people waiting for their friends to come out of the toilet waste a few dollars here.

If you think a slot is tight, follow your instincts and move to the one next to it. Casinos never place two loose slots side by side.

PLAY THE MAXIMUM NUMBER OF COINS

Many machines give you the option to choose how many coins you want to stake for each play. Always play the highest stake, otherwise you lock yourself out of the biggest jackpot. If the slot is progressive (the jackpot increases with each play) and you are staking less than the maximum, you are increasing the pot for everyone else, without being eligible to win it yourself.

SET GOALS

Decide what you want from your gaming. How much do you want to spend and how long do you want to play? If your bankroll is $200, always walk away when you've lost it. Or if you decide you want to be entertained for an hour, walk away after an hour, regardless of how much money you've got left.

DON'T GET GREEDY

The slot's brain is merely a random number generator, so your chance of winning the jackpot is the same each time you play, regardless of how long you have played. Aim for medium range gains, rather than pumping more and more money in because you think you are inches away from the big payout. A machine is never "due for the big one" because the payback percentage is worked out over the long term. For the same reason, don't assume that because a machine seemed loose for you one day that it will automatically pay out for you tomorrow.

KNOW YOUR MACHINE

There is no point in playing a slot that you don't understand. Why reduce your odds of winning with ignorance? Watch someone else play until you understand the machine.

45. TP A HOUSE:

There isn't really a wrong way to TP a house, short of forgetting to bring any toilet paper, trying to throw it in pouring rain, or getting caught. However, here are a few pointers.

BUYING SUPPLIES

If you are under the age of twenty-one, then going to the supermarket checkout with a hundred rolls of the cheapest and least butt-friendly toilet paper in the Western world is bound to raise suspicion. Get a homeless person or a retiree to buy it for you, so you don't incriminate yourself. Buy the TP several days before the event (and at least two weeks before your school's homecoming football game/graduation, because many stores won't sell toilet paper to adolescents in the days leading up to these events). Better still, purchase small quantities over time to create a stockpile.

WHICH TOILET PAPER SHOULD I CHOOSE?

Obviously you shouldn't waste the likes of aloe vera impregnated Charmin triple ply on a TP mission, but equally, if you buy stuff that is too thin the paper will snap when you throw it. Achieve a balance between TP that's strong enough to stay together versus the limitations of your budget. We recommend Kirkland TP which can be bought cheaply in packs of forty-eight from Costco.

TP TIME

The best time to TP is at night (or during a total solar eclipse) and the later the better. The best time is around 1:00 A.M. because most people are asleep by then.

PICK A HOUSE

Ideally choose the house of someone unpopular. You also want a lawn that has a few large trees, because that's where you'll be delivering the goods. You can throw paper over the roof, but it's not nearly as effective as up a tree. Make sure all the lights are out inside the house.

Throwing technique

Grip the loose end of the paper in one hand and then throw the roll as high and as far as you can over the top of the tree. Walk to the other side of the tree and pick up the roll and throw it again. Repeat ninety-six times, or until you run out of toilet paper. Trail TP over bushes as well. Rip up lots of small pieces of TP and scatter them over the lawn. Do all this quickly and silently and you won't get caught (remember, TP'ing is technically an act of vandalism).

46. BASE JUMPING:

The behavior that separates humans from other animals is that some of us seem to enjoy exposing ourselves to unnecessary risks. BASE jumping, which involves using a parachute to jump from fixed objects (rather than from an airplane) is one sport in which this peculiar trait can be expressed.

WHAT DOES BASE STAND FOR?

BASE was coined by a moviemaker Carl Boenish in 1978, neatly summing up the sort of locations from which you can expect to hurl yourself: it stands for **B**uilding, **A**ntenna, **S**pan (a bridge, arch, or dome), and **E**arth (a cliff or other natural formation). Critics of the "sport" point out that it can also stand for "**B**ones **A**nd **S**hit **E**verywhere." Unsurprisingly, BASE jumping's illustrious founder died on a cliff jump in 1984.

HOW IS IT DIFFERENT FROM SKYDIVING?

First, it's much more dangerous. It is recommended that you perform at least 150 skydives before attempting your first BASE jump. BASE jumps are usually made from much lower altitudes

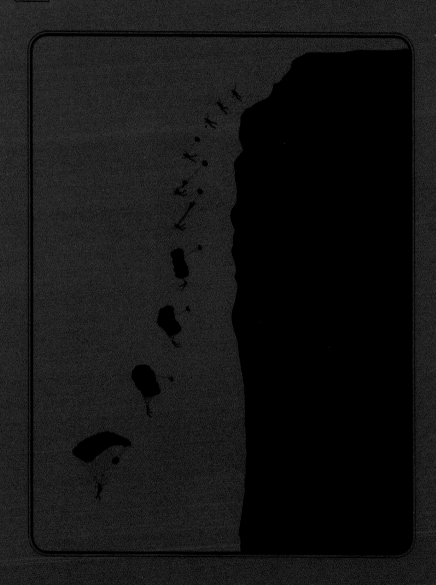

than skydives, although the current Guinness World Record for a BASE jump is from the 19,000-foot Trango cliff in Pakistan.

Skydivers use air flow to stabilize their position, so that they can open their parachute cleanly. BASE jumpers rarely reach terminal velocity, and therefore have less aerodynamic control, making chute deployment more hazardous. You'll also need a special parachute (and no backup—no time to use it), one that is bigger with a large pilot chute, and you'll only have a few seconds of freefall before chute deployment.

WHERE CAN I JUMP?

BASE jumping itself isn't illegal, but the trespassing you'll have to do to reach some of your jump platforms is. There is only one man-made structure in the U.S. where you can BASE jump legally year round: Perrine Bridge in Twin Falls, Idaho. Once a year, however, on the third Saturday in October, it's "Bridge Day" at the New River Gorge Bridge in Fayetteville, West Virginia, where over 800 jumps are made in a window of just six hours. Other than that, if you want to jump from the Sears Tower, it's up to you to get to the top without being arrested.

APPLY FOR A BASE NUMBER

When you complete a jump you can apply for a "BASE number." The first (BASE-1) was awarded to Phil Smith of Houston, Texas, in 1981.

47. BECOME A FAKE MEDIUM:

Here are some of the good old fashioned tricks that fake mediums used in their heyday. Incredibly these methods succeeded in fooling thousands of Victorians into parting with their cash in the belief that they were witnessing the manifestations of dead spirits.

DIM THE LIGHTS

Always perform your séance in a dark or nearly dark room. Tell your clients that this makes it easier for the spirits to manifest.

SPIRIT CABINET

Hide all your magic tricks, props, and costumes in a large piece of furniture that has hidden compartments, or in a curtained-off area of the room. This is your "spirit cabinet." Explain that this will help you to attract, channel, and conserve spiritual forces. Allow your clients to view the cabinet, but make sure that the last person to inspect it is your assistant, who will plant the necessary equipment. Keep more wigs and makeup in a fake panel in your chair.

GHOSTS

Get your assistant to materialize from a trapdoor in the floor or a sliding panel in the wall, or pretend to be a dead child by walking around the room on your knees.

MOVING OBJECTS

Floating spirits can be made by painting faces on inflated balloons. Attach objects by a fine thread to an adjustable fishing rod to make them move.

SPIRIT MUSIC

Getting the spirit to play a musical instrument is an important part of the show. For example, make a violin play eerie notes by dangling a weight from a thread off the end of the table. The thread then passes over strings of the violin and then through the keyhole of a door, where it is pulled back and forth by your assistant in the next room.

HOLDING HANDS

Holding hands around the table ensures that you cannot use them for trickery. However, if everyone alternates hand/wrist, then after the lights have gone down it is easy to make your neighbors believe they are each holding one of your hands, when in fact, they will be holding the hand and wrist of the same arm, leaving the other free for wielding your fishing rod, etc.

ECTOPLASM

Spirit forms are made of "ectoplasm," which is a weird wispy substance that often emanates from a top-notch medium. Make fake ectoplasm from egg white, mixtures of soap, chewed paper, silk, or cheesecloth. Secrete it inside your mouth, and pull it out and wave it around at an opportune moment.

48. BREAK BRICKS WITH YOUR HANDS:

Breaking bricks with your hands requires impeccable technique and considerable mental focus. The three basic principles are having self belief, hitting the brick as fast as possible, and minimizing the contact surface of the blow to maximize force.

STANCE

With the soles of your feet firmly on the ground, bend your knees to lower your center of gravity. This is the solid base from which you can generate the power and speed to break bricks.

INTENSE FOCUS

Place both of your hands on the surface of the brick, and focus intently on the point through which you intend to strike. Aim for a target underneath the center of the brick. Maintain this eye contact until your hand has smashed through the masonry.

SPEED AND FLUIDITY

Move fast and with natural ease. Raise your striking hand backwards behind your head in a natural arc, while keeping your other hand on the brick. This is your backswing: it focuses your energy and keeps you fluid.

Turn your hips away from the target, and then bring them back again to transfer this torque energy into a striking force. Slice downward with a karate-chop hand as fast as you can in a natural arc, and tighten the muscles of the hand as it slices through the surface of the brick.

As your striking hand comes down, drive the other hand backwards in a circular movement to balance your body and to increase your power.

CONTACT SURFACE

The part of your hand that makes contact is the small bone just below your little finger (the fifth metacarpal). Human bone can withstand forty times more stress than concrete, while the muscle, tendons, ligaments, and soft tissue in the hand disperse the energy of the impact up through the arm so that you do not injure yourself.

The more momentum your hand has, the more force it can generate, and when that force is delivered through a small point of contact, it is concentrated with devastating results.

49. BUY A PORN MAG:

Since the arrival of screen-to-screen Internet porn, buying a jizz mag feels as quaintly redundant as Route 66. The prurient depiction of sexual acts printed on compressed wood pulp feels not a little out of date, and in years to come no doubt these six-fist catalysts will be so rare that copies will only be handled by reference librarians wearing masks and white gloves. Buying one used to be the scariest thing that a young man could do, but today this rite of passage seems set to escape an entire generation.

CHOOSE YOUR LOCATION CAREFULLY

The size and busyness of the shop is important. If the shop is too small, you may have been the only customer that day, and your purchase will assume a significance that it doesn't warrant. If the shop is too busy, you'll have to stand in a line, and people will know that you're planning a one-man show. A shop that is somewhere in between these extremes means that you can buy your mag during a lull, but the shop assistant will be too busy to care much about your reading preferences.

KEEP BROWSING TO A MINIMUM

The longer you browse, the greater the likelihood that someone you know will walk in. If another customer approaches, ditch your copy of *Wet Shaved Lesbian Teens* and pick up something harmless like *Autotrader*, otherwise you could cause offense.

MAKE OTHER PURCHASES

Always buy another magazine or newspaper as well as your smut, otherwise it will seem like the only reason you climbed out of bed that morning. Your porn should appear almost like an afterthought: you can take it or leave it. Better still, buy a packet of condoms, then the shop assistant will think your girlfriend has sent you on an errand to bring back forty-eight pages of girl-on-girl action to get her in the mood.

AT THE CHECKOUT

Place the magazine face up so that the price is clearly visible. You don't want the shop assistant spending ages waving it around in search of a bar code. You need it scanned, paid for, and bagged in under three seconds. Using the correct change also shaves vital seconds off the transaction time. Then hurry home and take a load off your mind.

50. EXERCISE YOUR SQUATTER'S RIGHTS:

In the U.S., squatting laws vary from state to state, but usually your presence won't be tolerated for very long. The legal property owner and/or neighbors will inform the authorities, and then the police will bust your ass for trespassing and kick you off the property. However, there are a few things you can do to tip the scales in your favor.

ENTERING THE PROPERTY

There are two types of squat: "back window" and "front door." In the first, you come and go without being seen so no one knows you are there. In the second, you don't make any effort to hide your comings and goings.

When entering the property for the first time, do not leave any signs of forced entry. Breaking into a house is a criminal offense (such as forcing locks, breaking windows, etc). However, unscrewing a padlock bracket and then hiding it is not. The burden of proof will be on the owner to prove that there

was a lock there. It is unlikely that he will have taken photographs of it.

HIDE THE TRESPASSING SIGNS

Remove and hide any signs which warn against trespassing.
Again, the burden of proof is on the owner to show that all
reasonable efforts were made to alert trespassers that they
are unwelcome, and if you plead the Fifth, even though everyone knows that the signs were there, they can't prove that you
saw or removed them. However, you will still be considered a
trespasser against the owner. In legal terms, what you are
doing is called "adverse possession" which is a form of civil
trespass unless you fulfill certain legal requirements.

STAY FOR A LOOONG TIME

To keep a property you must continuously possess it for
several years (this varies from state to state) against the
owner's will and pay all the property taxes.

As a squatter, you have no rights as a tenant, but you do
have a Constitutional right to "due process of law," which
means that the owner will have to take you to trial before you
can be evicted, so long as the police don't rule that you are
in the process of breaking and entering and remove you. Don't
cause any criminal damage because you may be forced to pay
damages to the owner.

51. FIVE THINGS YOU SHOULDN'T DO WITH AN EGG:

1. Throw them at politicians. It's a well-established form of humiliation and civil protest, and it is probably written into the Constitution somewhere.

2. Collect them from trees, cliffs and other inaccessible places. The rarest bird's egg in the world comes from the rarest bird in the world: the Spix's macaw (a long-tailed, all blue parrot), which is native to Brazil. There aren't any left in the wild, but there are a few in captive breeding programs.

3. Keep your cocaine in it. Supermodel Kate Moss allegedly used to travel the world hiding her stash in a $100,000 Fabergé egg without getting caught.

4. Culture your own personal supply of anthrax bacteria.

5. Keep them in one basket.

52. FREE RUNNING (PARKOUR):

Free running is often called *Le Parkour* (sometimes abbreviated as PK) or *art du déplacement*. They're not strictly the same thing, because free running grew out of *Le Parkour*, but what the hell. Let's call them the same thing and really annoy those French guys who invented it.

WHAT IS IT?

It's a physical art (and philosophy), the aim of which is to travel from point A to point B while overcoming obstacles as efficiently and quickly as possible, using the abilities of the human body. Male parkouristas are known as *traceurs* and females as *traceuses*. It was invented by Frenchman David Belle, whose main inspiration came from the "Natural Method of Physical Culture" developed by Georges Hébert in the early twentieth century and used by French soldiers in Vietnam. Belle says that the spirit of *parkour* is guided by the ideas of "escape" and "reach," combining quick thinking and dexterity to get the practitioner out of difficult situations. Trust the French to invent the martial art of running away. However, this is running away with efficiency and style.

GETTING STARTED

Parkour is not made up of a list of fixed moves, like gym-
nastics. It is more fluid. Each individual must find their own
unique way of overcoming each obstacle, depending on their
body type, agility, and the nature of the obstacle itself. The
most important skill to learn is good jumping and landing
techniques, because lots of *traceurs* injure their joints by
dropping and rolling incorrectly.

SOME MOVES

Always land on your toes and bend your knees, and in
higher jumps transfer vertical energy into forward momentum
by rolling. Develop your balance by walking along the crest
of obstacles, and practice precision jumps from one object to
a precise spot on another object. Master the underbar jump
(under and through a bar or a gap between obstacles). Then
there's the hanging drop, vault (jumping over stuff), pop vault
(overcoming a wall, usually by kicking off the wall to turn
forward momentum into upward momentum), turn vault (involv-
ing a 180° turn), reverse vault (jumping over stuff with a 360°
rotation), and the gap jump (jumping over gaps).

STYLE NOT MACHISMO

All the time you are developing your skills, think French:
you're aiming for style and efficiency, not trying to show off
or be macho. For instance, jumping a gap and not falling to
your death is all very well, but it's more important to jump
with style. The French would rather die than look unstylish.

53. ANNOY YOUR NEIGHBOR:

Eric Hoffer said, "It is easier to love humanity as a whole than to love one's neighbor." Fortunately, it's real easy to make your neighbor's life a living hell.

1. Paint cuss words on his immaculate front lawn using weed killer. In a few days, the grass will turn brown and die, and your profanities will magically appear.

2. Staying on the weed killer theme, sneak into your neighbor's backyard and paint a circle about six feet in diameter. A few days later when the grass has died, stick a stake in the middle of the circle, then shave bald patches on their dog and tie it on a short leash to the stake. Call animal welfare.

3. Put up a sign outside their house saying "ALL BROKEN FRIDGES GRATEFULLY RECEIVED," or have a garage sale to sell off their stuff while they are away on vacation.

4. Find out where your neighbor shops and buy exactly the same outfits. Always wear them one day after your neighbor does.

5. Every time you see your neighbor washing his car, gardening, cleaning out his garage, etc., say "How would you like to do mine when you're finished?"

6. Keep yelling at imaginary kids to "Be quiet! You'll disturb the neighbors."

7. Begin a fifteen-year construction project on your house.

8. Float unwrapped chocolate bars and toilet paper in your neighbor's pool.

9. Make him think his car has an oil leak by pouring a little oil under the engine every morning.

10. Block his drains with human remains.

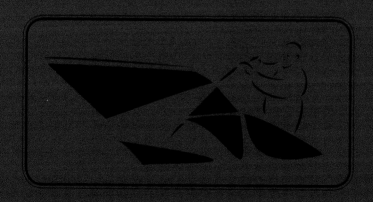

54. PAINLESS PARENTING:

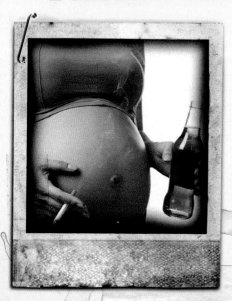

Bringing up kids in the modern world is 99 percent perspiration and 1 percent gratification. It's often frustrating, always exhausting, and rarely worth all the effort. But it doesn't need to be this way. Put yourself first. Yes, believe it or not, psychologists now admit that the best parenting is *lazy parenting*, because if you're not happy, your kids sure as hell won't be. So go on, reach for another beer, pick up the remote control, and let them know that hey . . . you've got needs too!

ARM WRESTLING

Take every opportunity to arm wrestle with your children. This will teach them how to lose with dignity and lets them know who is boss. Stop when they are big enough to beat you up.

BRIBERY

Bribery is not an effective method of disciplining children. Use blackmail instead.

CHILDREN LOVE SURPRISES

Children get bored easily, so liven things up by creating a fun and totally unpredictable household. Cook them dinner any time between four and midnight. Come home from work at a different time each day. Promise to take them to Disneyland then forget you ever mentioned it. Lose your temper, then laugh hysterically. Kids just love to be kept on their toes.

HONESTY

Always be honest. For example, if your child does something stupid, make eye contact and say "You are really stupid." Then give them constructive advice: "Do it like this, stupid . . ."

I WANT

Avoid pester power by giving your children anything they want. The novelty will soon wear off, and when they're sixteen they'll renounce capitalism and become a priest or nun. That way you avoid the really big expenses like a car, wedding, etc.

I'M ONLY HUMAN

Children need to know that their parents are fallible. Show them it's OK to make mistakes by shagging your partner's best friend, developing a drinking problem, and getting your house repossessed. This will make your children happier and more confident.

IMAGINARY FRIENDS

Any child who tells you that she has an imaginary friend is pulling one over on you. To prove it, wrap up an empty box for her birthday and tell her it's an imaginary Play Station 3. The imaginary friend will soon make a swift disappearance.

INDEPENDENCE

Foster independence in your young children by sending them out to buy you cigarettes.

LOVE

Kids love to be helpful and they love to be loved. Foster a feeling of love in your children by starting sentences with "I'll love you if . . ." For example: "I'll love you if you fetch me a beer . . . I'll love you if you do the washing up . . . I'll love you if you take the trash out."

MAKING MISTAKES

Let children make their own mistakes. That way you can stay on the sofa and have a good laugh at their expense.

RAIN

When your child wants to know where rain comes from, tell him that God is crying because of something he did.

ROLE MODELS

Foster a sense of healthy competition between your children by constantly comparing them to one another. Begin sentences with "Why can't you be like . . ."

SOCIAL AWARENESS

Help your children develop a social conscience by taking them into the nearest city to spot homeless people sleeping in doorways. Explain that many people become homeless because of an intolerable situation at home. Remind them of this fact every time they get on your nerves.

TANTRUMS

When a child is very angry, he will often want to get even. Why not encourage him to express his feelings by breaking into the house of the person who has angered him and spraying on the walls a list of all the horrible things that he wants to do to that person. He will soon recognize the absurdity of his behavior, his anger will disappear, and he'll return home laughing ... no harm done.

55. PICK-POCKETING TECHNIQUES:

The great benefit of pick-pocketing is that you can earn thousands in a few hours without the need to mug people at gun point. Also, some of your victims won't even know they've been robbed, and they will blame themselves for leaving their purse in a shop. If you are thinking of pressing up against a few people in the subway, here are some pick-pocketing tips to get you started.

DRESS AGAINST TYPE

What's your mental picture of a pickpocket? He is probably a scrawny male scumbag between the ages of sixteen and thirty. But this picture is wrong. Many pickpockets dress to resemble the type of people you would least expect to rob you: wealthy businessmen, tourists, and middle-class mothers with babies.

OPPORTUNISM

Often it doesn't take much skill to steal a purse or mobile phone. Go to any crowded public area and you'll see people sitting around with their bags unattended. A guy who sticks his wallet in the back pocket of his pants or in the outside pocket of his loose-fitting coat is practically asking for it. Carry a jacket or newspaper to cover your hands while you work.

DISTRACTION

Your greatest weapon is distraction. Pickpockets often work in groups, so that while one or more members of the gang cause a distraction, the other one lifts the victim's belongings. Here are some common distraction techniques:

1. Have a fight with one of your accomplices, while the other members of your gang steal the belongings of those who gather to watch.

2. One of you accidentally drops the contents of your handbag all over the floor. When a kind person squats down to help pick things up, another gets busy in her pockets.

3. Go to any place where there is a ready-made distraction, such as street theater. The crowd there is easy pickings.

4. The "stall" stops suddenly in front of your victim, so that another member of your gang (the "pick") bumps into them, and steals their wallet, while making a big deal of apologizing. The mark will not suspect the pick because their attention (and possible irritation and frustration) is focused on the stall.

FOLLOW THE MONEY

Announce to your friend in a loud voice "Someone stole my wallet!" The reaction of those around you will be to pat their own wallets to make sure they are still there. Perfect. Now you know where they keep their valuables. Also, watch people at ATM machines and shop checkouts to see where they put their wallets and purses when they leave. Also, you can brush past them to feel for the bulge their wallet makes (this is called "fanning").

56. SOBER UP QUICKLY:

Unfortunately there is no quick way to sober up—not cold showers, fresh air, or black coffee. Alcohol will stay in your body until it is broken down by your liver and eventually leaves your body through breath, sweat, and urine.

HOW DOES ALCOHOL WORK?

When you drink alcohol, it enters the bloodstream through your stomach and intestines. Then the bloodstream carries it to other parts of the body and it reaches the brain almost immediately. Alcohol is a depressant so it gets to work immediately inhibiting brain function.

Time is the only thing that can sober you up. Your liver needs time to break down the alcohol. The body can metabolize half an ounce of ethanol per hour. A standard drink contains just under half an ounce of ethanol, so you must allow about one hour for every standard drink you consume.

That said, there are a few things you can do to create the illusion of sobriety:

EATING FOOD SLOWS DOWN ALCOHOL ABSORPTION

Food slows the absorption of alcohol into the bloodstream (but eventually the alcohol will be absorbed and impairment will occur). Nevertheless, if you've just had a few drinks, eat some fatty food and your body will absorb the alcohol more slowly. In effect, this is the reverse of sobering up, since the alcohol stays in your body longer, but you will stand more chance of seeing the evening out.

DRINK REGULARLY TO INCREASE YOUR TOLERANCE

Hardened drinkers increase their tolerance to alcohol. Several years of regular drinking actually trains your liver to break down alcohol more efficiently, with the added bonus that your brain cells become less sensitive to its effects. This won't affect your blood alcohol concentration (so you will still fail a Breathalyzer if you're over the limit), but it will make you feel less drunk.

KEEP YOUR PANTS ON

There's nothing guaranteed to make you feel more drunk than trying to remove your pants at the end of the night. You can feel in control right until the moment when you stand on one leg and end up face down on the carpet. Go to bed in them.

DRINK LOTS OF WATER

Drink lots of water to help your liver get rid of the alcohol. It also reduces the chances of you getting a hangover, which is most often caused by dehydration and vitamin deficiencies.

57. TEN HABITS OF HIGHLY EFFECTIVE MEN:

1. Don't call, ever.

2. If you don't like a girl, don't tell her. It's more fun to let her figure it out by herself.

3. Women like it when you ignore them. It turns them on.

4. If you are forced into a situation where you have to talk to a woman on the phone, use only one-syllable words. Tell her you're missing the football game.

5. A general rule: If whatever you're doing does not satisfy you completely in five minutes, it's really not worth it.

6. Women hear best with their breasts, so make sure you're looking at them when you speak.

7. If you're going out with someone but you love someone else, don't say anything. Wait until the woman you are dating falls in love with you, and then tell her.

8. Have strong opinions on everything, especially sports and immigration.

9. Practice your blank stare.

10. If you are ever forced to show emotion, just pick ones like rage, lust, and insanity, and display them at random, inconvenient times. You won't be asked to do it again.

58. TEN HABITS OF HIGHLY EFFECTIVE WOMEN:

1. If asked what you look for in a man, always reply "a sense of humor." Then when you marry an eighty-year-old millionaire, your friends will understand why you can't stop smiling.

2. Only date men whose salary is four times greater than their age.

3. Inject collagen into your lips. Men love dating women who look like they've just run face first into a wall.

4. Rather than reaching into your closet for your shoes, just buy another pair.

5. Spend half an hour each day exfoliating rather than practicing how to parallel park.

6. Don't worry about filling the car up with gas or checking the oil. If the pistons shoot through the hood, it was just meant to be.

7. Pretend to be scared of insects, spiders, and small rodents. Insist that he kills any that come within fifty feet of you.

8. Roll up your used tampons and leave them on the windowsill in the toilet. It's not healthy for him to put you on a pedestal.

9. Gain twenty pounds then expect him to switch off his latest Vin Diesel DVD to shag you like a weasel.

10. Insist that he is present at the birth of your children. Watching the combined contents of your uterus, colon, and lower intestines shoot out of your ass will be a day he'll cherish for the rest of his life.

59. ESCAPE FROM PRISON:

Only consider a jail break if you are on death row or serving a life sentence with little chance of parole. Otherwise, you would be wiser to do your time, unless conditions inside have become intolerable for other reasons, such as your having recently become another prisoner's bitch or your broker needs a signature before he can offload some more pharmaceutical shares. It is worth considering the consequence of a failed escape attempt: solitary confinement, an increase in your sentence, or drowning in the freezing waters of San Francisco Bay.

METHODS OF ESCAPE

If you are disorganized or lack the necessary temperament to plan and execute a getaway over several months, you would be more suited to an opportunistic escape: a door left unlocked, a faulty electric perimeter fence, etc. However, you may have to wait a long time for such an opportunity to present itself, time better spent tunneling a hole behind the toilet. Also, if you consider that the odds of one door being left unlocked is a hundred to one, then if you have to get through five doors to reach freedom, your chances of all five of them being unlocked at the same time is one in ten billion. To put this into perspective: you're two million times more likely to die in the first thirty days after a total knee replacement surgery.

If, on the other hand, you are a meticulous planner, good with your hands, and a perfectionist problem-solver with an eye for detail like Martha Stewart, you should opt for a planned escape. If nothing else, your single-minded focus on breaking out will give you a sense of hope and purpose that is so often lacking in correctional facilities.

GETTING HELP

Whether you dig a tunnel, hide in a laundry sack, or start a riot, most prison breaks require assistance from others either inside or outside the prison. Those on the outside—friends and family—you can trust. However, getting people to help you in prison requires considerable interpersonal skills, and you must be prepared to forgo some of your luxuries (e.g., your toilet paper and cocaine ration) so that you can use them to bribe other inmates or even a prison guard to assist you and to keep quiet.

PLAN B

If your escape plan fails, just continue to be clothed, fed, and housed by the state until massive federal budget cuts force the release of hundreds of prisoners.

60. THE ART OF TREPANNING:

If you or a loved one has become possessed by an evil spirit or demon that is causing an illness or disease of some kind, your first step is to thrash, starve or torment the individual in an attempt to drive the spirit out to search for a more hospitable host. If that fails and their condition persists, you may be forced to follow the lead of generations of ancient man: trepanning. This is a process by which a section of the top of the skull is carefully removed so as to promote mental and physical well-being.

The ancients used trepanning with some success: many skulls show that the bone continued to grow around the hole, indicating that the patient did not die from the procedure. Trepanning was used for centuries to treat conditions as varied as common headaches to epilepsy and more serious mental disorders. With the advent of modern power tools and drugs, this procedure is considerably easier than it used to be.

Here's what you do:

1. Concoct an ointment from herbs that are known to have a mild anesthetic quality, for example kava kava.

2. Apply the ointment generously to a small area at the top of the skull.

3. Cut away a flap of skin with sharp flint tools and fold back; do not cut away completely as you will need this later.

4. Make a series of small round holes in the skull with a power drill so that you have traced the outline of a small circle (if you want to be more traditional and "unplugged," use a hand-cranked drill specifically designed to pierce the skull).

5. Cut between these holes with a pair of pruning shears until you have removed a section of the top of the skull completely.

6. Pay careful attention not to cut too deeply: you are not aiming to remove brain tissue, simply bone.

7. After surgery, stitch back the skull and cover with a sterile gauze to prevent infection. Allow your patient several months to recuperate.

61. CRASH A WEDDING:

There are three common reasons for attending a wedding without an invitation: stealing food, getting laid, and mingling with celebrities. You may even hit pay dirt with the holy grail of wedding crashers: lucrative paparazzi shots.

STEALING FOOD

This is probably the least ambitious motivation for the wedding crasher, and may not even be cost effective. If you've had to spend several hundred dollars on an outfit to blend in with the wedding party, it is unlikely that you can recoup your initial expense, no matter how many salmon terrines you manage to stuff into your handbag. If a free meal ticket is your main goal, hit low-budget, low-class weddings, and accept that instead of lobster thermidor and caviar you are more likely to encounter quiches, sausages on sticks, and deviled eggs. On the plus side, there's no need to hang around for the wedding speeches. In a high-class wedding, pretend to be one of the caterers, because after you've spent eight hours on your feet serving, you'll get to finish off the vol-au-vents and other uneaten high-brow food (of which there will be plenty).

GETTING LAID

Everyone knows that weddings are the place to get laid by horny bridesmaids. Dressing up a pretty young single woman in pink crinoline and forcing her to watch her best friend joined in holy matrimony is a surefire recipe for making her feel unloved and over-the-hill. That's why all bridesmaids are up for it, but it's also why you should avoid them: every other guy in the place will be hitting on them, leaving all the other females to fall for your charms.

THE CELEBRITY WEDDING

Don't feel guilty about crashing a celebrity wedding. Sell your photographs to a national glossy magazine and everyone benefits: the magazine pays you a fortune, its circulation increases by a couple hundred thousand, and the celebrity couple sues them for $2 million for stress, loss of income, and damage to their professional careers.

THREE WEDDING CRASHING TIPS

Now you know *why* crashing a wedding is good news, here are three hows:

1. Wear a kilt if you're a man, or take along a baby and breastfeed it if you're a woman.

2. If the wedding clashes with an important sporting event, bring a portable radio and keep the male guests abreast of the score.

3. If you sit in Madonna's seat, don't pretend to be Madonna.

62. AVOID BUBONIC PLAGUE:

Bubonic plague is an infectious disease that has caused many epidemics throughout history. It is most commonly transmitted to humans when they are bitten by the rat flea after it has fed on a rat infected with the disease. Symptoms include high fevers, aching limbs, vomiting of blood, and swollen lymph glands (buboes) in the armpits, neck, and groin which eventually burst causing death. There are many ways—medical and religious—to reduce the risk of catching the plague.

MEDICAL PRECAUTIONS

1. Burn incense (juniper, pine, beech, rosemary, camphor and sulfur) to ward off deadly vapors exhaled by the earth.

2. When walking outside, cover your face with a handkerchief that has been dipped in aromatic oil.

3. Purchase spells, talismans, and charms from your apothecary or wise woman.

4. Drink elderberry juice every day and wear a jade necklace.

5. Avoid eating poultry, waterfowl, pork, old beef, fish, and anything that has been cooked in rainwater.

6. Do not sleep during the daytime and avoid too much exercise and bathing.

7. Address your thoughts to pleasant and agreeable things: beautiful landscapes; melodious songs; and gold, silver, and other precious stones. Don't think about death.

8. If you are wealthy, flee to the countryside.

RELIGIOUS PRECAUTIONS

1. Go to confession regularly to confess your sins.

2. Self-inflicted suffering and penance are effective ways of lessening divinely inflicted suffering. So perform numerous penitential acts such as pilgrimages, self-flagellation, processions, fasting, and giving money to the poor in order to lessen God's wrath.

3. Ring church bells and fire cannons to drive the plague away.

63. CUT OPEN ANIMALS TO PREDICT THE FUTURE:

Extispicy is a form of divination practiced by the Babylonians and later by the Romans and Greeks. It involves slaughtering an animal (usually a bull) and examining the entrails to determine whether a particular endeavor is advisable. It is derived from the words "extra" and "spiere" meaning to view or consider.

Extispicy works on the principle that when an animal is slaughtered, it is absorbed by the god to which it has been offered. Opening up the animal to examine the viscera is akin to gazing into the mind of the god in order to see how the future will play out.

1. Pay special attention to the liver—it is the smoking mirror of Heaven. Examine the pyramid-shaped projection called the *processus pyramidalis*.

2. Burn the animal on a sacrificial pyre and examine the way the flames burn in order to prognosticate further.

3. Examine cracks in the scapulas of the bones as they burn (scapulomancy) and look for omens in the cooled ashes (tephromancy).

AUSPICOUS SIGNS

A large *processus pyramidalis* is a good sign. It should be well-formed and free from imperfections.

INAUSPICOUS SIGNS

The following are ~~signs of~~ impending doom:

A cleft *processus pyramidalis*

The heat of the fire is waning (the same thing happened just before the death of Julius Caesar when two oxen were burned on an insufficient pyre)

The person presiding over the ceremony accidentally drops the entrails

The viscera are unusually bloody or are of a disturbing color

A missing *processus pyramidalis*

64. TEN THINGS YOU SHOULDN'T DO WITH A HAMSTER:

1. Scrape its teeth slowly down a blackboard to annoy your friends.

2. Clean it. Hamsters are smelly little creatures, but they are supposedly self-cleaning. So bathing it in water is an ideal way to ensure it catches a cold and dies.

3. Stop it from eating its own feces. It's a disgusting little rodent habit designed to absorb nutrients that its digestive system missed the first time round.

4. Marry it. A guy in Boulder, Colorado, tried to marry his horse a few years ago, and a woman in India allegedly married her dog, so why draw the line at hamsters? Be warned that the pre-nup will probably be ruled inadmissible when you divorce, and the hamster will walk away with your house.

5. Turn photos of your pet into personalized Christmas gifts for your friends and family. Nobody wants hamster aprons, calendars, coasters, hats, license plate frames, boxer shorts, lunch boxes, stickers, or toilet seats.

6. Don't insert it up your backside without shaving it first (the hamster), otherwise you will experience a painful build-up of electrostatic electricity.

7. Give it a face lift and it will starve to death. Hammy needs those baggy pouches in the side of his face to carry all his food.

8. Use it to run electric cable along a cavity wall.

9. Don't wrap it in Scotch tape; use masking or electric insulation tape, which peels of easily after sex without removing too much fur.

10. Don't expect them to give you any pleasure. They are nocturnal and about as much fun as a badger.

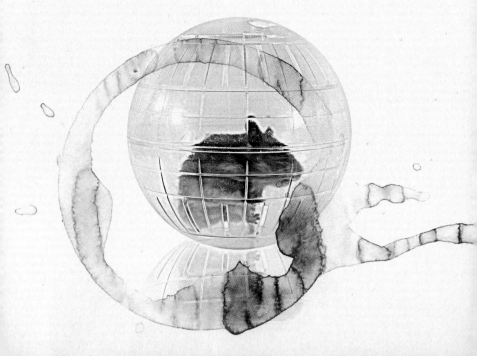

65. LIBEL SOMEONE:

Libel is the defamation of an individual, business, product, group, government, or nation in a published work (photos, words), with malice aforethought resulting in damages to that person's/institution's/nation's reputation and/or livelihood.

WHAT IF YOU'RE TELLING THE TRUTH?

If you can prove that what you have said about them is true, then it isn't libel. Also, if you say something in good faith which you believe to be true, without malice, it isn't libel. There has to be knowledge of falsity or a reckless disregard for the truth, as well as malicious intent.

MALICE AFORETHOUGHT

Until 1964, a person could prove that they had been libeled simply by showing that the statements in question were false. In 1964, the Supreme Court decided that public officials had to prove that the statements in question were made with "actual malice" in order to damage the person's reputation.

HOW DOES LIBEL DIFFER FROM SLANDER?

Slander is a harmful statement in a transitory form (such as speech) whereas libel is in a fixed medium: writing, photo or picture, sign, or electronic broadcast, etc. Both libel and slander are forms of defamation.

THE INTERNET

You can also libel someone on the Internet. In the U.S., you can only be sued once for each e-publication, whereas under European and Commonwealth jurisdictions, you could be sued in every country in which your e-publication is read.

FINANCIAL DAMAGES

If libel is proved, then the harmed parties can only claim financial damages if they can prove that they have suffered a financial loss as a result of the libel (e.g., loss of reputation leading to loss of business). If someone's reputation and position in society is already very low, it might be ruled that they are "libel-proof," since anything that you can say against them can't make them sink any lower than they already are.

66. DRINK A YARD OF FABRIC SOFTENER:

Downing up to four pints of fabric softener from an "ell glass" while a crowd of your friends offer drunken encouragement and support may seem like an end in itself, but learning how to imbibe without spilling a drop actually requires a bit of skill.

The "ell glass" takes its name from the "ell"—a measurement of one yard and nine inches. The yard of ale was ubiquitous in English taverns during the seventeenth century; its shape enabled the glass to be handed to highwaymen sitting atop horse-drawn carriages, so that they needn't disembark.

Spillage—the bane of all ell glass drinkers—can be avoided by recognizing that when the glass is tilted, air is prevented from getting into the bottom bulb until the drinker has raised the glass high. Then it suddenly gushes out.

1. Hold the neck of the glass in your left hand (in your right if you are left-handed) and reach down as far as you can to the bulb end with your other hand. The further you reach, the greater your power of leverage and, hence, your control of the glass.

2. To prevent a rush of fluid: lift, tilt, and twirl. Lift slowly, tilt the glass slowly as you drink, and twist the glass so that air reaches the bottom gradually.

3. Some yardies prefer to twirl the glass quickly to create a vortex that uses centrifugal force to keep the fabric softener at the outside of the glass so that it slides into the throat more easily. Fast or slow—use whichever method works best for you.

4. After you have downed the liquid, raise the empty vessel aloft and give a hearty cheer. You should now have a soft, fresh, static-free stomach.

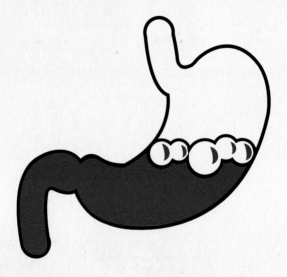

67. HANG, DRAW, AND QUARTER:

It was the British who introduced the torture of hang, draw, and quarter as punishment for the crime of treason. It was first used by King Edward I in 1283 on the Welsh prince Dafydd ap Gruffydd. It was thought to be the cruelest form of capital punishment and was only used on men.

1. Make sure that the felon is male. If the subject is shown to be a female, she should not suffer to be hanged, drawn, and quartered, but should instead be burned at the stake. This method should only be used for high treason. Petty treason is punishable by mere hanging without dismemberment.

2. Tie the criminal to a wooden frame and drag him through the streets to the place of execution. This allows the townsfolk to verbally and physically abuse him, each according to their own desires.

3. First, make a noose and hang the felon by his neck.

4. If the felon has paid you handsomely, make sure he is dead before proceeding to the next stage—the "drawing."

5. If the felon has failed to bribe you, cut open his abdomen so that his innards fall onto the floor while he is still alive.

6. Hold the entrails up and display them to the assembled crowd.

7. Cut off the genitalia and burn these together with the viscera in plain view of the dying victim.

8. After he is dead, take him from the scaffold, behead the corpse, and cut the body into four pieces—this is called "quartering."

9. Display each of the five body parts (the four quarters and the head) in different prominent positions around town as a deterrent to other would-be traitors— this is called "gibbeting."

68. PLACE A GYPSY CURSE:

Can you rokra Romany?
Can you play the bosh?
Can you jal adrey the staripen?
Can you chin the cost?

Can you speak the Roman tongue?
Can you play the fiddle?
Can you eat the prison-loaf?
Can you cut and whittle?

A gypsy curse can either be an insult or the effective action of some power, distinguished solely by the quality of adversity that it brings. Three conditions have to be met in order for your gypsy curse to work.

1. You must believe that the person you are cursing has transgressed an acceptable code of conduct. You can't curse someone if they've done nothing wrong.

2. The person you have cursed must be made aware that they have been cursed.

3. They must also believe that you have the power and responsibility to lay a curse on them.

Here are some choice gypsy curses to get you started, but it is more effective to invent your own:

1. "May you wander over the face of the earth forever, never sleep twice in the same bed, never drink water twice from the same well, and never cross the same river twice in a year" (this is probably the most famous gypsy curse in the world).

2. "May your daughter's hair grow thick and abundant, all over her face."

3. "May the IRS disallow all your deductions."

4. "May the fleas of a thousand dead camels infest one of your errogenous zones."

5. "May your every wish be granted."

6. "May your left ear wither and fall into your right pocket."

7. "May you get slightly fatter every year."

69. PERFORM AN EXORCISM :

If you are looking for a medical explanation for an individual with unnatural behavior, look no further than the seventeenth century's favorite diagnosis: demonic possession.

1. Find yourself an exorcist and check his credentials. In medieval and early modern times, the exorcist was a lower-ranking priest—one who had not yet successfully completed his Holy Orders. Today, exorcists are quite the opposite—they are senior and widely respected figures in the Roman Catholic Church. In either case, the exorcist can only face the devil head-on if he has the full authority of the Roman Catholic Church.

2. The exorcist will select one or more assistants who may be other priests or laypersons, each of whom must swear to carry out the exorcist's commands and instructions immediately without question. They must also make a full confession before the exorcism so as to be as free as possible from the guilt of sin that the devil will inevitably use against them.

3. Finally, you need to reach the conclusion that exorcism is the only means of saving the poor soul. The exorcist will need to place the possessed person in a room in which they are generally most comfortable and feel most secure, often their own bedroom.

4. The room is cleared of anything that could potentially be moved, hurled, or thrown: inexplicable telekinesis and flying objects are a real safety hazard.

5. Windows and doors must be sealed so as to contain the force of evil within as confined a space as possible.

6. Equipped with a crucifix, Holy Water, two candles, and a Bible, the exorcism begins. No one addresses the devil directly at any stage. The exorcism is a sacrament with a set pattern. The exorcist must adhere strictly to this if the devil is to be driven out. The process may last for days, and it continues without significant breaks until the devil is finally ousted.

70. STREAK AT A SPORTING EVENT :

Streaking is usually defined as "the non-sexual act of taking off one's clothes and running naked through a public place." Therefore it is important while you are cavorting around naked that you don't do anything that can be interpreted as overtly sexual, such as taking yourself in hand, sitting on the umpire's face, or getting an erection. Streaking should be harmless fun. Sure you'll get arrested and heavily fined, but that shouldn't stop you from relishing your five minutes of fame. Above all, remember to smile.

CROWD PLEASER

Remember you are primarily streaking for your own enjoyment and to show off to your friends. If the crowd is with you, then that's a bonus. The reception you receive from the crowd is dependent upon whether you are male or female. Male streakers are usually treated with contempt by the players, but for some reason the sight of a nice pair of funbags generates considerably less hostility.

CAN I AFFORD IT?

Be aware that in recent years broadcasters have been discouraged from filming streakers, so it is unlikely that you will appear on TV, as the camera will cut away the moment you appear. However, the fine for streaking has increased considerably, so you might want to consider copying Lisa Lewis, who sold her bikini on trademe.com after streaking at the Waikato Stadium in 2006 during a rugby match between the All Blacks and Ireland.

PICK YOUR MOMENT

Leave at least half an hour between eating a large meal and streaking, as the crowd wants to see the bouncing beauty of the human body, not the contents of your stomach.

Time your streak so that it doesn't interfere with direct play, for example, while the field goal kicker is lining up for an extra point, or while a soccer player is taking a free kick. Never strip when the Pakistan cricket team is playing Ireland. It takes a lot of concentration to deliberately lose a match and your unwelcome appearance could easily throw them back on their game; the last thing you want is to get on the wrong side of criminal gambling syndicates.

While streaking and certain sports just don't go together (Nascar racing, global yacht racing, and bobsledding spring to mind), don't feel you have to restrict yourself to streaking at baseball and football games. In January 2000, twenty-two-year-old waitress Tracy Seargant ran naked down the green of the Indoor Bowls Championship.

71.RABBIT POACHING:

If you live in a trailer park and spend all your money on cable, booze, and cigarettes, the ability to snare a rabbit can be the difference between hardship and hunger. Here's how to set a simple twitch-up snare.

TWITCH-UP SNARE

A wire snare is best for small animals such as rabbits. Use 20-gauge wire and twist one end into a loop, then fold the loop back so that it forms a double loop. Pass the other end of the wire through the two loops to form a noose.

1. Bend back a branch to form the twitch-up mechanism.

2. Make the trigger mechanism as in the diagram.

3. Make sure that the loop is high enough above the ground so that it catches only the rabbit's head and not a foot. When the rabbit runs through the loop, it tightens around its neck; as it continues to run forward it knocks away the sticks making the large branch swing upwards, lifting the rabbit into the air.

PLACEMENT

Set up your snare in a place where you know rabbits are. Look for runs, trails, tracks, and droppings. Also look for bedding areas, watering holes, and feeding areas that are linked by trails.

CONCEALMENT

Not only must your trap be concealed from view, but, more importantly, from smell. When you are setting your trap with your hands, you will leave human scent on it, which is a powerful warning signal to alert your prey. Conceal your smell by covering your hands with soil before handling the trap; alternatively, you can coat the trap with rabbit urine from a previous kill. Another option is to smoke your trap. Try to disturb the vegetation around the trap as little as possible.

BUILD A CHANNEL

Building an inconspicuous funnel of twigs and branches is a good way to channel the prey towards your trap. Once the animal has entered the funnel it cannot go left or right, and it is still more likely to continue into the trap rather than turn around.

BAIT THE TRAP

Use a bait that the rabbit is familiar with, but not something that is too abundant in the area. The bait should be a treat.

72. TEST IF SOMEONE IS A WITCH :

There are several ways of finding out if someone is a witch, all of them based on the presumption that the unfortunate subjects are guilty until proven otherwise.

SCALES TEST

Place the witch on one arm of a huge set of scales. On the other arm place a metal bound copy of the Bible. If the suspect weighs more than the Bible, she is innocent and should be set free. If she weighs less than the Bible, she is a witch.

If you are convinced that the suspect is a witch or if she looks particularly heavy, hide extra weights inside the Bible so that she fails the test regardless.

LOOK FOR WITCHMARKS

All witches have unusual markings on their body that are signs of the Devil. These include birthmarks, warts, and moles, and they are places where the Devil suckles from the witch to regain his strength.

Once you have located a suspected witchmark, prick it with a pin. If this does not draw blood or cause pain, this is confirmation that it is a genuine witchmark.

DROWNING TEST

Bind the suspect, right foot to left hand and right hand to left foot, and throw her into the local river or pond. If the suspect floats, then she is a witch and should be hanged. If she is innocent, she will sink and most likely drown.

A dunking stool may also be used for this purpose. This is a wooden diving chair. Strap the witch securely into the chair and dunk her in a pond. The length of the dunking is entirely up to your discretion—lasting anywhere between a few seconds to several hours. If the suspect is an old lady, the shock of the cold water may be sufficient to kill her, thus proving her innocence.

TORTURE

Subject the suspect to horrific torture until she confesses to being in league with Satan.

73. WARD OFF EVIL SPIRITS:

There are many ancient ways of warding off evil spirits and protecting yourself from the evil eye.

1. Make extensive use of gargoyles as a design feature on your house. Their ugly faces and grotesque expressions scare away evil spirits.

2. Use an amulet to provide protection against harm. It can be worn around the neck or kept in your pocket, and it can take many forms including protective hands, fish, angels, diamonds, written charms, human finger bones, tiger's teeth, rabbit's feet, goat's feet, Egyptian scarab, arrowheads, knuckle bones from a piece of mutton, pine cones, and toads.

3. The use of certain plants and herbs is effective, such as agrimony, anise seed, aloe, angelica, basil, caraway seeds, fennel, garlic, hazel, majoram, willow (good for magic wands), vervain, and wintergreen. Scatter tea leaves in front of your house.

4. Bless someone when they sneeze.

5. When you spill salt, throw a pinch of it over your left shoulder (that's the side of your body where evil spirits dwell).

6. A yawn is a sign that Death is summoning you, so cover your mouth when you yawn or evil spirits will enter your body through it.

7. Tying knots in your handkerchief helps you to remember something because a knot is a charm against evil.

8. When baking, remember to mark your loaves with a cross.

9. Mummify a cat and brick it up in the wall of your house.

10. Hang a horseshoe above the door. Evil spirits linger in doorways. That's why a bride must be carried over the threshold.

11. Drip wax from a Paschal Candle between the horns of your livestock to protect them from disease caused by evil elves and witches.

12. Kill any hen that persistently crows before it destroys its eggs and teaches other hens to do likewise. It has the Devil inside it.

13. Whenever you ahear the hoot of an owl, put irons in your fire, or throw salt or vinegar into the fire; or remove your clothes, turn them inside out, and put them back on.

14. Ring bells and bang pots and pans after a wedding ceremony. The bridesmaids dress up finely to act as decoy brides and confuse evil spirits.

15. On Friday the 13th, walk around your house thirteen times.

74. THE ETIQUETTE OF DUELING:

When someone insults you, either reach for your weapon and teach them some manners, or elect to settle the dispute like a gentleman, with a test of courage, nerve, character, and personal honor: pistols at dawn.

DEMAND SATISFACTION

Challenge someone to a duel by demanding "satisfaction" from them accompanied by an insulting gesture. In past times, this was usually slapping them in the face with a glove, however, mooning or giving them the bird is also acceptable. If they decline the challenge, they must issue a personal and, in some cases, a public apology.

APPOINT A SECOND

Appoint a trusted friend to be your "second." His first job will be to liaise with your opponent's second to see if the dispute can be settled amicably without the need for a duel. Before the duel, your second is responsible for loading your pistol and ensuring that your opponent isn't cheating (e.g., by wearing concealed body armor or using an assault rifle). If you are unable to take part in the duel, your second should stand in for you.

PISTOLS AT DAWN

You and your opponent begin back to back, at dawn (usually on a grassy knoll, next to a gnarled old tree surrounded by swirling mist). Since a duel is a private affair between the two individuals concerned, only they, their seconds, and a referee should be present. One of the seconds (or referee if you have one) calls the order "March," the duelists walk an agreed number of paces, then turn and fire.

If you fire and miss, you must allow the other person to take their shot. If they choose to fire in the air, rather than at you, they win the right to refuse future challenges.

The duel can either be to the death or can be called after first blood has been drawn. In other words, the first person to bleed loses.

75. SURVIVE IN A FOREIGN JAIL:

You disembark from the airplane after a grueling long-haul flight. All you want to do is get to your hotel, take a bath, and sleep for twelve hours. No such luck. There's a welcoming party of grim-faced drug officers waiting to drag you off to jail. You should have packed your own bags, you moron. Now what do you do?

Here's how to survive your own nightmare version of Midnight Express.

THEY HANG DRUG SMUGGLERS, DON'T THEY?

Some do (Turkey, Thailand, Malaysia, Singapore, Indonesia, Iran, and Algeria), but many countries have mandatory prison sentences ranging from seven years to life, without the possibility of parole for drug violations. Unfortunately, there is very little that anyone can do to help you if you are caught with drugs. If you've told someone at home when to expect you back, you have a chance that they will report you "missing" to your embassy. You can't rely on "one phone call" in a foreign lockup situation. So you'd better shut up and do your time.

CONTACT THE U.S. EMBASSY

If you are arrested and are carrying a U.S. passport, you have the right to contact the American embassy immediately. When an American has been arrested or detained, the local police are obliged to contact the nearest U.S. embassy.

WHAT CAN AN EMBASSY OFFICIAL DO FOR YOU?

So long as they know where you are, they can visit you in jail; they can give you a list of local lawyers (but they can't assume responsibility for their integrity—in other words, they could be crooked or incompetent); they can notify your family and friends; and they can intercede with local authorities to insure that your rights are being observed (under local law, that is—these may well be very different from what you would expect at home).

WHAT CAN'T AN EMBASSY DO?

It can't demand that you be released and expatriated, nor can it represent you at trial, give legal advice, or pay any fines or legal fees.

CASH AND CIGARETTES

On the inside, cash and cigarettes are essential commodities; they can get you anything from better food (instead of starvation rations) to protection and even sex. Using these as bribes may even get you released.

LEARN THE LANGUAGE AND GET TO KNOW PEOPLE

If you get thrown in for a long time, learn the language, culture, and customs of the people, and use that knowledge.

KEEP YOUR HEAD DOWN

You may be a mule, but don't be a donkey as well. The last thing you need is for the goon squad to single you out as a troublemaker. If you want to have the crap beaten out of you or spend weeks naked in solitary confinement with nothing but a filthy mattress, go ahead and act like a big shot. If you're sensible, stick to the rules and don't do anything to get noticed.

76. BECOME A COMPUTER HACKER:

So you've decided to become a computer hacker but you don't know where to start. The most important quality a hacker needs is curiosity, because this fuels the development of your skills. If you're a person who instinctively wants to know how things work, likes stripping stuff down and building it up again, and loves problem-solving, then you have the beginnings of the hacker mindset.

You don't become a hacker overnight. It takes years of dedication and of soaking up information from every possible source: books, the Internet, newsgroups, etc. Back in 1996, a hacker named Eric Steven Raymond wrote a web document about hacking that many hackers consider definitive: see www.catb.org/~esr/faqs/hacker-howto.html for an updated version.

1. Learn how to program. Start with Perl in Unix, or Visual Basic and Java in Windows, though hacking in Windows is very limiting. Then learn C, the core language of Unix, and move on to C++, which is closely related to it. The more programming languages you learn, the more

options you'll have because you can compare how they work, and each language is suited to different tasks. The best way to learn a computer language is to immerse yourself in the environment and use it, contact others who are using it, share code and ideas, and live and breathe open source software.

2. Learn how to run an open source operating system like Unix/Linux. Install Linux or one of the BSD-Unixes and install it on a personal machine. Then you can play around without destroying your other work. Unix is the operating system of the Internet, so you have to know it to be able to hack.

3. Learn about data communication, networks, and how computers talk to each other. The best way to learn about the World Wide Web is to learn HTML and write lots of web pages.

4. Get out there in the hacker community; go on newsgroups and talk to people, join user groups and contribute to the group (rather than just asking "How do I hack?"). Share what you learn and others will share with you. No hacker is an island. To be part of the hacking community you have to identify with its goals and values, which you can only learn and attach importance to by becoming involved.

5. Set yourself projects and follow through with them. If you write a bit of code that solves a specific problem, share it with others.

6. Never stop broadening your knowledge and allowing your curiosity to guide your learning.

7. If you're a true hacker, you won't need any of this advice, because you'll already be doing it.

77. BUILD FREAKISH MUSCLES:

Irrespective of age and gender, every physique has the capacity to build big muscle, provided it is trained and given rest at proper periods. There are countless build-rock-hard-muscle formulas on the Internet, promising guaranteed satisfaction or your money back, accompanied by pictures of guys who have added thirty pounds of muscle in just twelve weeks. Ignore them. Here are some genuine muscle-building tips to help you get awesome and ripped.

1. Allow your body adequate time to recuperate between training sessions. One of the pitfalls of "hard gainers" (those who build muscle slowly) is overtraining. Go to the gym for an hour, three to four times a week. Never go two days in a row. This allows your body time to rest, keeps you from getting bored, and enables you to be more focused when you are working out.

2. Perform low reps with high weights, but remember that good form is more important than the amount of weight you are lifting. You can only target muscle if you can control

the weight. If your dumbbell curls look like jerks, you've got bad style. Lower the weight and stop trying to impress other gym users.

3. Use free weights instead of machine and cable exercises.

4. Surprise your muscles and keep your training fresh by varying the exercises, the number of reps, the tempo of the reps; and by gradually increasing the weight every couple of weeks. You've got to mix things up to make maximum gains. Train to total muscle failure on at least a few sets every workout.

5. Don't waste time training your abs to get a six pack. Fat is burned all over the body when you train, not just in certain areas. Lose weight and your six pack will appear.

6. Eat at least two grams of protein per pound of body weight. If you weigh 150 pounds, you need to eat at least 300 grams of protein. Eat a small meal every two to three hours.

7. Drink at least eight glasses of water a day and get at least eight hours of sleep each night.

8. Inject yourself daily with HGH (Human Growth Hormone), a 191-amino acid, single chain polypeptide that occurs naturally in the human body and is produced by the pituitary gland. What's the worst that can happen? Your bones growing out of shape and heart disease? A small price to pay for freakish muscle growth.

78. COMPLAIN AND GET RESULTS:

What do you do when things haven't gone according to plan and you want to complain? Perhaps you want to return a broken product, a service has been unsatisfactory, been kept waiting, or received poor customer service.

You might seek financial compensation, a replacement item, or merely an apology. If you kick up a fuss, lose your temper, and make life very uncomfortable for everyone, you may well get what you want, but equally you may alienate those who are trying to resolve your problem.

The best strategy is to smile, stay calm and polite, explain the problem clearly and briefly, and make allies not enemies.

1. Start the conversation with the assumption that the other person wants to resolve your problem (which is usually true—most of us like to please). Right away you will feel more positive and cooperative and less antagonistic.

2. Make sure that you are talking to a person who has the time and, most importantly, the authority to help you. There's no point spending twenty minutes explaining your grievance to the janitor. Ask to speak to someone in authority. In general, the higher up you go, the better your chances of a favorable and speedy result. Many complaints are resolved swiftly as soon as they have been brought to the attention of a senior manager.

3. Always get the name of the person you are talking to, especially when you are on the telephone. Keep a record of the time and duration of each call and what was discussed or agreed.

4. Make clear that you do not blame the other person for the problem. It is your job to get them on your side so that they will be more inclined to help you.

5. Explain your situation calmly and quietly. Keep you body language open and relaxed, and on the phone talk rationally and politely.

6. Try to talk about the matter objectively rather than being emotional. You need the other person to fix your problem, not change your mood. Getting emotional or threatening will usually cause the other person to feel blamed and defensive.

7. Smile. Who would you think was more assertive—a person who states what they want while smiling or frowning? You can smile and still mean business. People respond more favorably to your smile because it shows that you are not a physical threat.

8. Once you've got someone to listen to your complaint, make sure that you thank them for taking the time and effort to help you. Also, make it clear what result you are expecting.

9. End the conversation with a question that invites empathy with your situation. For example say something like "I'm not being unreasonable, am I?", "I'm sure you can understand why I am upset?", or "You'd do the same in my position, right?" It is hard for an employee to answer "no" to direct questions such as these without sounding unhelpful. It's a subtle way to press them into your service! A smile or nod as you say it will reinforce it even further.

10. Whatever the outcome, thank the person again for their time. If you didn't get a resolution, ask for the name and contact details of someone more senior. Make sure you get the name of the person who originally helped you, so that you make it clear to them that you are holding people accountable and mean business.

79. DOGGING RULES AND ETIQUETTE:

Dogging is engaging in sexual acts in semi-public places such as parks or parking lots, or watching others do so. The craze started in Great Britain, is spreading around the world, and is coming soon to a town near you! However, before you jump in your car and head for the nearest beauty spot, here are a few rules to bear in mind.

1. **Doggers hook up on Internet forums and newsgroups, many of which post a time and a place, or else rely on text messaging to keep the location a secret. Alternatively, you could go to a likely venue and put out a general shout on your Bluetooth mobile to anyone in the vicinity. Whatever you do, don't drive aimlessly around a dogging spot looking for action as you will attract law enforcement and spoil the fun for everyone.**

2. **Look out for a car with flashing headlights or an interior light. This is an invitation to come and view some action.**

3. **When you're crowding around a car, don't block the view for other doggers.**

4. Hands off unless invited to join in and be respectful to the women. Wear a condom.

5. Clean up after yourself: remove condoms, tissues, underwear, etc. One sure way to get a dogging spot closed down by the cops is leaving trash for the general public to complain about.

6. Be aware of the law in your area. Part of the fun is doing something illegal, but make sure you know whether or not you are breaking the law, so you can make a choice.

7. If you are inside a car, lock your valuables in the glove compartment, and keep the door locked, unless you want to invite someone in to join you.

8. Leave the engine running so that you can make a quick getaway if the cops arrive.

9. Angry local residents may try to disperse you with fake police sirens. These pesky killjoys are called "Roys."

10. Dogging in a luxury automobile is known as "poodling."

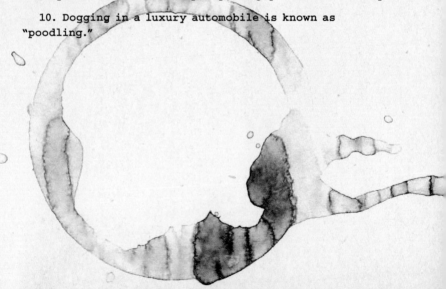

80. FAKE AN ORGASM:

Before you decide to fake an orgasm you'd better decide where you see your relationship heading. If you're on a one-night stand and want to get done with the humping, it's not hard to see the benefits of a little deception. However, if you're in for the long haul, do you really want to encourage your partner to continue pressing all the wrong buttons by reinforcing their behavior with a colossal faked climax? It's your choice, but accept that this trickery may be the first of many.

It has been said that women can fake orgasms, but men can fake entire relationships. In fact, research shows that plenty of men fake orgasms, too.

WOMEN

Some women argue that their men are so inattentive that a quick moan and a couple of pants is enough to fool them into thinking that they have ridden the rainbow. However, if your man needs a little more convincing, follow these steps:

1. Try to copy what you would normally do when having an orgasm. If you usually cum quietly, putting on a noisy show just won't feel right.

2. Twitch a little and tighten and release your vagina over and over again to simulate the internal pulse that happens during an orgasm.

3. Curl your toes and bite the pillow.

4. Tense your body as you "climax" and then relax again afterwards.

5. If none of the above work, just imagine you are having the most astounding sex with someone else, and make a mental note to acquaint your partner with your clitoris at the earliest opportunity.

MEN

Why do guys need to fake it? Surely they can cum whenever they like? Not if they've already jerked off six times that day or drank too much alcohol.

1. You can't fake ejaculation but it is possible to fake the pelvic contractions that accompany it. Imagine you wanted to wave your erection up and down without using your hands, you'd do it by sort of tightening your sphincter. It's the same when you're inside a woman. A few of those, accompanied by some serious face pulling and muscle tensing in the rest of your body should do the trick.

2. Afterwards, think of something really unpleasant to get rid of your boner, because your cock's supposed to go flaccid after ejaculation, remember? If this doesn't work, you may have to claim that you're on Viagra, but then she might want to go again (although the chances are she faked her orgasm too and just wants to go to sleep).

81. FIGHT LIKE A BOUNCER:

The best bouncers are personable, friendly, and skilled at talking to people to defuse a potential fight diplomatically and without appearing threatening or intimidating. However, when you need to pummel some faces, here are some golden rules of bouncing.

1. You've got to be able to take as much punishment as you can dish out. Otherwise, you will get seriously hurt, even killed. The first ten seconds of a fight are crucial. Take control of the fight immediately and stick together with your bouncer friends no matter what.

2. You need to end the fight as quickly as possible, and if that means putting the other person in a coma, so be it.

3. When you're working a door, you have to jump in at the first sign of trouble, otherwise you will never work as a bouncer again. If you don't pull your weight, no one will want you on their team.

4. Only work with bouncers that you trust and respect, otherwise you will all end up bleeding in the gutter. Only work with those whom you know will take a blade or bullet for you.

5. Don't show any fear. The moment your enemy can see fear in your eyes is the moment you are beaten and will have the crap kicked out of you. You have to know 110 percent that you are unbeatable.

6. Work out where the surveillance camera blind spots are so that you can kick people unconscious without fear of prosecution when the cops arrive.

7. If someone is really messed up and unconscious when the cops arrive, tell them he's one of yours (a bouncer).

8. If necessary, take the fight to the hospital to finish it off: it saves a lot of time in the long run.

9. Never back down from anyone. You have to be prepared to risk your life in order to save it.

10. However, if a big dude calling himself Kimbo wants to take you on, run back into the club, close all the doors, and don't come out until he's gone.

82. GETAWAY DRIVING TECHNIQUES:

If you've just robbed a bank (see page 230) and need to make a fast getaway, here are some useful techniques to evade capture by the authorities.

CHOOSE THE RIGHT CAR

You can use evasive driving techniques with most cars, but not jeeps or pickup trucks, as they can roll easily during heavy cornering. The best getaway cars are powerful, easy to handle, and reliable, like a BMW M5 or a Mercedes, with an automatic transmission and bullet-resistant, run-flat tires. Avoid high-performance cars like Ferraris and Lamborghinis—it is easy to lose control of these.

LOSING A TAIL

If you are being chased by cops, shake them off your tail by cutting across four lanes of traffic on the highway and take the exit (this won't deter a helicopter); or after turning a blind corner, turn 180 degrees using a handbrake turn (see page 218), then take off in the opposite direction.

TAKING CORNERS

When approaching a corner, taking a late apex enables you to exit the corner at greater speed than if you had taken an earlier apex. However, if you are being followed you run the risk of being overtaken on the inside.

KNOCK ANOTHER CAR OFF THE ROAD

If you are behind your victim, ram their bumper on the left side with the right side of your car. You should be traveling about 20 mph faster than the car in front. This will make the other car veer to the right and go into a skid.

Alternatively, you can run him off the road by pulling alongside his car to the right so that the center of your car is in line with his front tires, then steer left and press your car against his to steer him off the road. Needless to say, you should never let anyone pull up alongside you, as they will be able to perform these same maneuvers on you.

ROADBLOCKS

If you cannot escape a stationary roadblock by turning around, then you may have to ram it. To ram a two-car road-block:

1. Slow down, almost to a halt. This makes the cops think you are about to give yourself up.

2. Hit the gas suddenly and ram right in the middle of the two cars, maintaining your speed during the collision. Your impact speed should be between 15 and 30 mph.

3. After passing the roadblock, accelerate as quickly as possible and drive away.

83. GO AWOL FROM THE ARMED FORCES:

Armed service personnel are classed as going Absent Without Official Leave or AWOL when they are absent from their post without a valid pass or leave. The U.S. Marine Corps and Navy call it Unauthorized Absence, or "UA."

WHAT HAPPENS NEXT?

When you have been AWOL for thirty days, you will be dropped from your unit rolls and listed as a deserter. Under U.S. military law, desertion is not determined by the length of time a person has spent from the unit, but rather if there is a clear intent not to return or if there is intent to avoid dangerous duty or evade important responsibility. It's a clear indication you do not intend to return to your unit if you leave and then sign on with the same branch of service while keeping your previous unit a secret, or if you join a foreign armed force not authorized by the U.S.

TOP SECURITY CLEARANCE

If you go AWOL and you have top security clearance, you will automatically be classified as a deserter because of the sensitive nature of the information you had access to.

MISSING MOVEMENT

This is similar to going AWOL but is much more serious and is a violation of the 87th article of the Uniform Code of Military Justice. It occurs when you fail to arrive at a fixed time to deploy with your unit, ship, or aircraft.

YOUR PUNISHMENT

Before the Civil War, army deserters were flogged, and in the late nineteenth century they were tattooed and branded. The maximum U.S. penalty for desertion in wartime is death.

Persons considered AWOL/UA may be punished with non-judicial punishment (NJP; called "office hours" in the Marines). They are usually punished by court-martial for repeat or more severe offenses. However, if your father is a U.S. congressman from Texas and future President of the United States, then your superiors will never discipline you even if you blow off your military duties for seventeen months.

84. PERFORM A HANDBRAKE TURN:

The handbrake turn—changing direction by 180 degrees within the width of a two-lane road in a few seconds—is an essential evasive driving technique. It is also known as the bootlegger's turn as it is thought to have been used (if not invented) by hillbilly moonshiners to escape from revenue agents.

THE BOOTLEGGER'S/ HANDBRAKE TURN

It is much easier to perform this maneuver in a car that has an automatic transmission and a hand-operated emergency brake.

1. Reduce or increase your speed so that it is between 25 and 30 mph.

2. Take your foot off the gas and then turn the steering wheel about half a full turn, while simultaneously applying the emergency brake. If your car has a manual transmission, floor the clutch as well to keep the engine from stalling.

3. When the car is sideways, release the emergency brake, step on the gas, and straighten the steering wheel. With a manual transmission, let out the clutch as you apply the gas.

4. Speed away, but make sure you don't crash headlong into your baffled pursuers.

The bootlegger's turn punishes tires, so be sure to practice with your parent's car, a rental, or a stolen vehicle.

THE MOONSHINER'S TURN

This is a reverse bootlegger's turn, which uses similar principles while the car is traveling in reverse. It is an effective way of escaping from a roadblock.

1. Accelerate in reverse to a speed of 25 to 30 mph.

2. Take your foot off the gas, and then turn the steering wheel all the way to the left as quickly as possible.

3. When the car is sideways, shift from reverse into a low gear, straighten the steering wheel, and hit the gas.

4. Speed away, while ducking to avoid the automatic gunfire that will by now be pelting your back windshield.

85. GET EVEN WITH TELEMARKETERS:

Here's how to get back at those annoying sales people and have them running scared (well, they would run if they weren't chained to their desks).

If you are receiving unsolicited sales and marketing voice-recorded messages, and you have not given prior consent to receive such messages, you can ask the marketer to stop sending these.

They are legally obliged to act upon your request.

1. Register your phone number(s) with the National Do-Not-Call Registry at http://donotcall.gov. The organization is legally required to put your number on a "do-not-call" list, and to keep this information in their databases for ten years.

2. Whenever a telemarketer calls, tell them you want to be put on their "do-not-call" list. If you have already followed step 1, then they are breaking the law and you can take action against them.

3. Ask for the callers' full name, phone number, and name of the organization. Ask whether the organization keeps a list of numbers it has been asked not to call. If the answer is "no" to any of these questions, you may be able to sue them under the Telephone Consumer Protection Act for up to $1,500.

4. If you want to make things really difficult, ask for their supervisor and then demand that they send you a copy of their written policy concerning "do-not-call" numbers. The law requires them to supply this on demand.

5. Before hanging up, reiterate that you do not want to be called by them again, nor by an affiliate of their company.

6. If you're determined to litigate, spend $10 on a booklet called So You Want to Sue a Telemarketer, available from Private Citizen, Inc. by calling 1-800-CUT-JUNK.

86. START A RIOT:

Sounds like a tall order, huh? Not really. It's very easy to manipulate a group of people if you know something that they don't, and it only takes a few individuals to define the situation for everyone else. Of course, the best thing about a riot is that you get to break stuff and loot.

1. Get a bunch of your friends to dress as Los Angeles cops, then video them kicking the crap out of a black taxi driver. Post the footage on YouTube and watch the sparks fly.

2. Go to a march in Seattle and start smashing store windows. Soon local criminals will join the fray and start looting the downtown shops. The police will be poorly prepared and understaffed, and will be unable to stop the looters from running amok. Under pressure from federal officials, the city will declare an emergency and call in the National Guard.

3. Assemble a group of friends, dress up as activists, and attend a demonstration where there are lots of hardcore nuts, like animal rights protesters. Then get a couple of braver friends (who are dressed as police officers) to start pushing you around at a prearranged signal, using

unreasonable force. This will get the crowd jittery, so that the moment one of the "cops" accidentally kicks your dog, or steps on your hamster (which you have conveniently left on the ground), violence will erupt on the streets, and within half an hour you'll be enjoying a roaring spectacle as water cannon meets Molotov cocktail.

4. Go to a funeral service for victims who died in the last riot. There will be lots of tears and sobbing as well as rage and anxiety desperate for an outlet. All you have to do is throw a brick into a crowd of mourners and the whole thing will kick off.

5. Get a job in Starbucks in New York City. Wait for a killer heat wave and then offer free iced coffee to the first hundred customers.

87. SURVIVE AN ALIEN ABDUCTION:

You're driving your pick-up truck along a deserted road on a clear and still night, when suddenly you see a blinding light in front of you. Your car dies as several gray aliens start gliding towards you. What should you do?

DO NOT PANIC

Research has shown that 74 percent of potential alien abductees who panic end up scrambling up steep muddy inclines or running through impenetrable forest, only to be zapped unconscious.

DO NOT MOO OR CHEW GRASS

Do not do anything that might encourage the aliens to mistake you for a cow, otherwise you will find that your bowels and bodily fluids have been removed before you can say "ruminant mutilation."

RELAX

Let's face it—the aliens possess vastly superior intelli-
gence to you and no matter how tightly you clench your sphincter, they will find a way to insert a probe whether you like it
or not.

DON'T STAND OUT

Try to be as boring and "unevolved" as possible. For example, don't start juggling or show them that trick you do with
your tongue, or they might think that you are an unusual
specimen and cart you back to their galaxy.

FIDDLE WITH THEIR STUFF

Do you get annoyed when the children start playing with
your stereo? When they start pushing buttons indiscriminately,
it makes you want to shut them in the garden shed. Well, that's
precisely how aliens would react if you started showing a
primitive curiosity about their superior technology. Press a
few buttons and twiddle a few knobs in the control room. In no
time you'll wake up safely in your bed with nothing more than
a headache, a sore ass, and a couple of missing hours.

88. WHAT TO DO IF YOU'RE ARRESTED:

1. Stay calm and be polite and respectful. Don't resist arrest even if you know you are innocent, as then the cops can nail you for resisting arrest and are more likely to hurt you. Even if they start beating you up, don't resist, as this will only make them more violent.

2. Keep your hands where the cops can see them and don't make any sudden movements, like reaching into your jacket (or under the seat if you're in a vehicle). Don't give the cops any excuse to shoot you because they think you're going for your weapon. Don't touch a cop.

3. Only give the cops the names, addresses, and telephone numbers of yourself, your immediate family, and your employer; this information is needed for setting bail.

4. You have the right to remain silent. Anything you say may be used as evidence against you. The cops may try to get you to incriminate yourself by talking. Tell the cops you want to talk with a lawyer and keep quiet until he or she arrives.

5. The cops are allowed to search your vehicle if they have arrested you, or if they have probable cause that you have committed a crime (if not they need a warrant or your permission).

6. Try to memorize the physical appearance and badge numbers of the arresting cops, in case anything bad happens to you in custody.

7. You are allowed to make one phone call. Remember it may be bugged, so don't incriminate yourself.

8. If you think you have grounds for a complaint (e.g., wrongful arrest, police brutality, illegal search, etc.), keep quiet about it and concentrate on committing what is happening to you to memory.

9. You will be handcuffed, searched, photographed, and fingerprinted. If you're not released, your belt, shoelaces, wallet, jewelry, and other possessions will be taken away and kept in a sealed plastic bag by the jailkeeper.

10. You'll be locked in a cell while computer checks are run on your fingerprints to check for previous arrests or whether you are on probation. This could take up to twelve hours.

11. If you are charged with a misdemeanor, you can post bail at the station; if you are charged with a felony, you'll be taken to a bail hearing at the courthouse where a judge will decide whether you can be bailed out pending trial.

12. Don't plead guilty. Make the taxpayer pay to keep you in custody.

89. LIVE IN AN AIRPORT:

In the movie *The Terminal*, Tom Hanks plays a visitor to New York from Eastern Europe, who is stranded at Kennedy Airport after a civil war erupts in his country. He is unauthorized to enter the United States, but cannot return home, so he spends several weeks at the airport. How easy would this be in real life, and how badly do you want to get away from the local bums who hang out with you at the bus depot?

INVISIBILITY CLOAK

The biggest problem you'll face when bumming around in an airport is security. Short of wearing an invisibility cloak, there's not much you can do to avoid the surveillance cameras and security guards. You need to buy time by looking like a passenger who hasn't checked in yet. Carry a large suitcase stuffed with changes of clothes and various disguises, such as fake beards, glasses, and wigs. Every morning, dress up in a different disguise so that the security guards don't realize you are planning on becoming a semi-permanent fixture. Alternatively, wear a smart suit and a good pair of shoes, carry an attaché case, and talk loudly into your mobile phone. You will look like any another business-class traveler.

FINDING FOOD

All you've got to do is stay alive; anything else is a
luxury: that means getting hold of food and drink. Go to any
restroom and you can drink from the faucet for free. Forage
for food in a trash can, or hang around at the fast-food places
farthest away from the departure terminals—this is where the
most food is left uneaten because many passengers misjudge
their check-in time and have to leave in a hurry. If you're a
man, you need about 2,500 calories a day to live. Have a super-
sized Big Mac meal and we're talking about 1,500 calories right
there. If you can find a few coins in pay phones, you're set for
the day.

SLEEPING

You don't have to lock yourself in a bathroom stall to get
some sleep. Airports are open 24-7 and there are always people
lounging around looking exhausted and trying to catch some
shut-eye.

STAVING OFF BOREDOM

There are always lots of discarded newspapers lying around,
and when you've read the daily news, you can play games like
counting how many times you blink in one day.

90. ROB A BANK:

If you're not comfortable with computers, then holding up a bank the old-fashioned way with a gun and a stocking over your head will net you on average about $7,200 (according to the FBI). You are also more likely to get caught than an identity fraudster who sits at home on his PC and can steal thousands with a few clicks of a mouse. However, if you want to keep a dying art alive, here's what to do.

1. Stake out the bank for several weeks to observe its comings and goings, such as when the staff arrive and leave, when the busy and quiet times are, if there is a police presence, and when large shipments of cash arrive. Locate the surveillance cameras outside the premises.

2. Decide whether to use a real loaded gun, a real unloaded gun, a replica, or a toy gun. If you're caught, each category has different implications on your sentence, but don't assume the courts will be lenient just because you've used a water pistol. Also, if the cops arrive during your heist, you will be shot if you're brandishing any sort of weapon.

3. Better still, wear a dead man's switch that is rigged up to your heartbeat. This will trigger bombs that you have planted previously around the city the moment it detects that your heart has stopped (i.e., when you've been shot dead by the cops).

4. Enter the bank during the quietest time of day; cover your face as you enter, then put on a mask to disguise your face inside.

5. Pass the teller a note with your demands, and tell her to keep her hands in view so she can't press the emergency button.

6. When she has emptied her drawer of bills, stuff them down your pants and leave quickly, making sure that you aren't being followed.

7. Jump into your getaway vehicle, and, if in the unlikely event that you have made off with enough money to live on for the rest of your life, fake your own death and flee to a country that doesn't have an extradition treaty with the U.S.

IDENTITY THEFT

Dishonest bank employees will sell the personal banking information of customers for a price that depends on the amount of the funds in the account. If you want to steal millions, the banking details will cost you thousands, so you may have to rob a few banks the old-fashioned way first to build up some capital. Once you've got the bank details, you can take over the account and siphon off large amounts of cash.

Use other people's Social Security numbers and dates of birth to open accounts in their names to launder checks. If the police investigate, it's their names on the accounts not yours. For more about identity theft, see page 75.

91. RUN A PYRAMID SCHEME:

Pyramid schemes are illegal. They are "get-rich-quick" clubs which offer its members a large return on their investment, so long as they are able to recruit new members. However, these schemes quickly collapse and only those at the top make money. So why not be the one at the top? Here's how.

EXPLOIT GREED AND IGNORANCE

Pyramid schemes don't create money, they merely take it from those recruited later on down the line to pay those at the front of the queue. Fortunately, most people are blinded by greed and ignorance and don't understand that it would take an endless supply of new members to enable everyone who joined to see a return. As long as you don't draw attention to this, you're a winner.

THE LETTER

A pyramid scheme is the same as a chain letter, only money changes hands. Mail out a letter containing a list of six people's names and addresses (you and five friends) to a hundred people. The letter invites the recipient to "earn a windfall" and contains lots of enticing phrases like "Become part of the world's fastest growing industry" to convince them that this is an opportunity too good to pass over. All they have to do is send one dollar to the person at the top of the list (you), then cross out your name, slide the second person (your friend) to the top position, and add their own name and address in the bottom position. Then they need to copy the letter and send it to five friends. In return they will receive big bucks when their name reaches the top of the list.

THE PAYOFF

Of course, their name will never reach the top of the list, because if they understood statistics they'd realize that 48,828,125 people would have to take part before you and your five friends disappear from the list. Meanwhile, you'll all be busy booking tickets to an exotic destination to spend your hard-earned winnings.

92. START AN URBAN LEGEND:

An urban legend is a piece of modern folklore widely circulated by people who are enthralled by its content and who generally believe in its truth, or at least its plausibility. Urban legends aren't always untrue, but they are often distorted or sensationalized versions of real events.

Some urban legends have survived a long time, such as the story of a woman killed by spiders nesting in her hair or the one where the man woke up in a bath of ice with one of his kidneys removed by criminals who sold it on the black-market.

ESSENTIAL INGREDIENTS OF A SUCCESSFUL URBAN LEGEND

1. An urban legend can be as short as a single sentence or it can extend to a complete story with characters and a plot.

2. The compelling features that inspire the rapid spreading of an urban legend are mystery, horror, fear, danger, irony, or humor.

3. Many urban legends depict terrible crimes or include details of everyday items (such as contaminated food) that pose a threat to health. These myths are spread by people who feel compelled to warn others of the danger.

4. Some urban legends are extended jokes that are passed around as much for amusement or interest as for truth. An example is the hairdresser who attacks one of her customers because she believes he is pleasuring himself under the sheet, when he is merely cleaning his glasses.

5. They often contain a grain of truth: for example, the old lady who killed her wet cat by trying to dry it in a microwave oven (it's true that microwaving pets kills them, and that some old ladies don't understand modern technology).

6. Many urban legends warn of the danger of consumer products: eating Pop Rocks candy mixed with soda causes the stomach to explode, or that it takes seven years to digest swallowed chewing gum. Some persist despite the ease with which they can be disproved, such as the myth that a tooth left in a can of Coca-Cola will rot away overnight.

7. Many urban legends warn us of the illegal or underhanded behavior of major corporations, such as the KKK hidden on a pack of Marlboro cigarettes, or "under God" removed from the snippet of the Pledge of Allegiance printed on promotional cans of Pepsi.

LAUNCH YOUR OWN URBAN LEGEND

Drop your creation onto a message board, blog, or urban legend Web site and watch it grow. If it's a good one, you will see it spread across the world. Who knows, if it gains enough momentum, it might even end up on Mythbusters.

93. STUFF YOU SHOULDN'T DO IN A THEATER:

Actors are an insecure bunch. Most of them spend their lives below the poverty line, despising the job their doing if they're in work and hating "resting" when they're not. Meanwhile, they watch their suit-clad contemporaries who have endured proper jobs in offices climb the career ladder and achieve material comfort and social respectability. It is unsurprising then that theater types have developed a ludicrous repertoire of superstitions and rituals to help them feel in control of their lives. Here are some of the things you shouldn't do in the theater:

1. Shakespeare's play *Macbeth* is said to be cursed, so no one should mention it by name, either in a theater or in the presence of actors, whether they are in a rehearsal room or down at the bar. You should refer to it as the "Scottish Play." Actors also avoid quoting lines from the play, especially the witches' incantations. Anyone who says "Macbeth" must leave the room, turn around three times, spit, swear, and then ask permission to re-enter.

2. Whistling is considered bad luck. In times gone by, the theatrical rigging that controls the curtains and the stage flats were operated by stage crews who were often recruited from ships. Sailors and theatrical rigging crews used a series of coded whistles to communicate scene changes. Therefore, anyone whistling out of place could inadvertently trigger a scene change or find a heavy piece of scenery landing on their head.

3. Never wish an actor good luck. Instead say, "break a leg." One of the most common origins for this superstition is that during the time of King James I, the actors would line up on stage during the curtain call and if the audience was appreciative they would throw money (and later, flowers) onto the stage. Actors would then kneel down, breaking their leg line to pick up the money. Hence, "break a leg." In Spanish-speaking countries, the actors join hands before a performance and shout "Mierda!" (Shit!) for good luck.

4. Never leave a theater in total darkness. You should always leave a light burning in an empty theater, traditionally placed downstage center. This wards off ghosts and prevents injuries to the living.

5. Don't wear green clothes on stage unless absolutely necessary. In the 1600s shows were often performed outdoors on grass or in a field. Anyone wearing green would blend into the background.

6. Only wear blue clothes if you are also wearing silver. Blue dye used to be very expensive, so failing acting troupes would dye their clothes blue hoping to please the audience. However, if the actors could afford to also wear silver, it demonstrated that they were rich rather than desperate.

7. Don't use real money, wear real jewelry, or take peacock feathers on stage.

8. Never say the last line of a play in rehearsals. Save it for the first night in front of an audience.

94. SUBWAY SURFING:

Anyone can take part in the frighteningly dangerous and imprudent sport of subway surfing. Just jump on one of the thousands of trains that make up the New York City subway system, and then ride the waves for a few minutes until you drop to your inevitable death.

HOW TO SURF

The best surfing position is a snowboarding stance: spread your feet a little more than a shoulder-width apart, with one foot slightly in front of the other, and bend your knees.

Your front foot should face the front of the train, and your torso should face the side of the train. Keep equal weight on both feet and stretch out your arms for balance.

Look out for tunnels, bridges, and other overhead obstacles, and watch what the cars ahead of you are doing so that you can anticipate movement (e.g., watch to see if the train will turn left or right suddenly).

THE BENEFITS

1. You don't have to share the roof with anyone else or stick your face in someone's armpit.

2. You won't get pick-pocketed or mugged.

3. You won't have to breathe in other people's germs.

4. It's a great workout for your core abdominal muscles (mainly transverse abdominus and obliques), inner thighs, glutes, quadriceps, and calves.

5. Even people who can't swim can take part.

THE PITFALLS

The subway reaches speeds of up to 30 mph. It's hella dangerous; there are no safety harnesses and no instructors, so if you fall off you're probably going to die, or at the very least injure yourself bad. Still, what else have you got to live for?

95. TAKE PART IN A FLASH MOB:

A flash mob is a group of people who assemble suddenly in a public place, do something weird for a few minutes, and then quickly disperse. The first successful flash mob took place on June 3, 2003, at Macy's department store. It was organized by Bill Wasik, senior editor of *Harper's Magazine*. He claimed that he created flash mobs as a social experiment to highlight the cultural atmosphere of conformity.

More than one hundred people arrived at the rug department of Macy's and showed an interest in a particular expensive rug. When approached by shop assistants, all the participants said they lived together in a suburban commune on the outskirts of New York, and that they were collectively shopping for a "love rug."

WHAT'S THEIR PURPOSE?

What is the purpose of any act of random pointless? If anyone thinks they know the point, then they have failed to appreciate post-modern logic.

HOW TO GET INVOLVED

Flash mobs are organized by e-mail, online forums, and Web logs, and have taken place in major cities all over the world, from New York to Beijing. However, they are much rarer these days than when they were the hot ticket a few years ago. Then you could Google "flash mob" to quickly find an event in your area.

Why not organize your own event? The main headache is choosing a location that won't cause a problem, or break the law. As long as you keep the event brief and simple, it should be OK.

1. Think up an act of random pointlessness: such as a mass pillow fight or gathering around a sofa in a particular department store and saying "Oh, what a great sofa" etc.

2. Send an e-mail to about fifty friends and ask them to send it to another twenty friends.

3. If you want strangers (which is much better), set up a Web site and invite those who are interested to join a mailing list, so they can be informed of upcoming events.

4. Keep the actual details and precise location of the flash mob secret until everyone has assembled at four or five locations close to the event site, where they will be instructed to synchronize their watches and will receive slips of paper with details of the event.

5. It is vital that everyone disburses quickly afterwards and in an orderly manner.

Don't be too disappointed if no one shows up. It just means that people in your area have moved on. You may have to travel to a place where computerized social network interaction is still in its infancy. They say Mongolia is nice this time of year.

96. TALK YOUR WAY PAST A BORDER GUARD:

Everyone has heard horror stories about border crossing hell: bored soldiers with itchy trigger fingers waving large weapons around. Border posts can be very intimidating; roadblocks are a source of major stress, and visa offices can be a bureaucratic minefield.

However, more often it is the attitude of the traveler that dictates how they are treated. If you've got an attitude problem, expect to be given the protracted body (and vehicle) search. With some disturbing exceptions, bureaucrats and law and order officials in most countries are polite and friendly. In many cases where travelers fall foul of the law, they only have themselves to blame.

1. Don't assume that border officials are low-ranking civil servants. In many countries, they are very important government officials and must be treated accordingly.

2. Without going overboard, always keep a spare set of clean clothes for border crossings. The more respectable you look, the less trouble you will encounter. In many cultures, scruffy equals untrustworthy. Men should shave before crossing a border.

3. If you are wearing sunglasses or a hat, remove them as a sign of respect when you talk to the officials.

4. Keep your documents in an easily accessible place. If you keep the officials waiting, they will return the inconvenience in spades. However, never show your

impatience if you are kept waiting. The border guards have the power to refuse entry and turn you away. End of trip.

5. Even though many border stations only require one member of a large party to enter the post, it is good form (and good security sense) for everyone to get out, stick together, and present themselves for inspection.

6. If a guard approaches your vehicle, be ready to open the trunk. Keep it tidy, otherwise they'll have an excuse to pull everything out. Make sure one of your group stands guard to avoid theft.

7. If you want to engage them in small talk, a good icebreaker is to become involved in an impromptu language lesson. Officials are often bored and like to practice their English.

8. Stay calm and polite no matter how long you are kept waiting or how difficult the guards are being. If you lose you temper you will add hours to your ordeal.

9. Avoid crossing at busy times, such as weekends and public holidays, as you may have to pay an overtime fee, or you may be kept waiting until an overtime fee kicks in.

10. If you suspect that you are being asked for a bribe, pretend you don't understand or ask the person to accompany you to another office and to give you a receipt.

11. If traveling in a third world country, carry a few cheap pens in an outside pocket. If an officer asks to borrow one and admires it, offer it as a gesture of goodwill. It costs you pennies, but will buy you good favor without it being construed as bribery.

The rule of thumb is to play it by ear without putting your foot in your mouth—stay calm and respectful at all times.

97. BECOME AN ASSASSIN:

All you need to get started in the tough and glamorous world of contract killing is to place a classified ad that euphemistically expresses your gun-for-hire credentials. It is well-known in underworld circles that 60 percent of pest control adverts are actually selling the services of hit men: "Professional pest control: we have been helping homeowners, businesses, and deranged oligarchies solve their extermination problems since 1972. Send a manila envelope with your details to . . . discretion is our profession . . ."

When your first assignment comes in one morning, you're in business; it's time, as they say in hit man circles, to "go to work."

RIFLE ASSASSINATION

Your method of dispatching your target will depend on the weapons that you keep under your bed (all thanks to the Second Amendment). If you have a rifle, you can stay concealed and shoot from a distance; if you've only got a pistol, then you'll probably need to pose as a delivery person and gun them down when they open their front door wearing their pajamas. Any assassin who wants to be taken seriously should own a range of weapons, so we'll assume that you have a rifle.

The first rule of rifle assassination is to stay concealed. This means masking shiny or reflective items on your body and face (follow a regular skin-care regime to avoid oily patches), and eliminate unnecessary movement. Always go to the bathroom before a hit—you may not have another opportunity for several hours.

There are six basic positions of concealment: above, below, beside, behind, inside, and in front. Beware of silhouetting when you're on a roof or of getting trapped (never move into a space with only one escape route).

AIMING YOUR RIFLE

Grip the handle with your right hand and bring it up to your face. The rifle should be parallel to the ground. Place the barrel in your open left hand and then curl your fingers around it. Keeping the left arm bent and the elbow tucked into the body, raise the right elbow so that your arm is parallel with the ground, and tuck the rifle butt into the front of your right shoulder. Take aim.

Allow for the influence of wind and other factors that affect the fall of the bullet. Breathe steadily and normally, and do not hold your breath as you squeeze the trigger.

KEEP PRACTICING

Buy a video game system and practice killing for money: there are lots to choose from including *Oblivion*, *Hitman 2: Silent Assassin*, and *Assassin's Creed* to name but three.

98. CHEAT ON YOUR PARTNER:

Whether you are a man or a woman, it's time to face the fact that monogamy is unnatural. Sexual fidelity is virtually nonexistent in nature (sure, some species, mostly birds, are socially monogamous, but few are sexually monogamous). We all come from a long line of successful breeders and it is hard-wired into our genes to play away from home. Did you know that 85 percent of human cultures before the Judeo-Christian homogenization were polygamous? So what's the best way to do it?

1. **The most important rule is DON'T GET CAUGHT.** Cheated-on partners can do some extreme things when they discover they've been duped.

2. Don't date two people in the same city, otherwise you're bound to bump into one while out on a date with the other.

3. When you're on a date, always answer your cell phone; ignoring calls is a quick route to raising suspicion.

4. Develop a reputation in your relationships of being a bad liar; allow yourself to get caught lying badly over something trivial and your partner won't suspect that you could give lessons to Richard Nixon.

5. Be prepared for double-dating to take up twice your energy; eat healthily and exercise regularly: you'll need every bit of stamina you've got.

6. If you're living with your partner, never bring your affair home, as alien pubes in the soap dish or between the sheets are a dead giveaway.

7. When covering your tracks, always base your lies on the truth and pay attention to small details. Also, don't lie unless absolutely necessary: if you lie all the time, no one will believe you.

8. If your partner suspects that you're lying, burst into tears or break something.

9. Don't be tempted to spill the beans if your partner suggests a threesome or swinging; it may be a trap to make you fess up to your cheating.

10. If your partner discovers you've been cheating and you can't see yourself spending the rest of your life together, it is the ideal time to break free and get out. There's no point acting all repentant and spending months trying to rebuild trust for a relationship with no long-term future.

99. COMPETITIVE FREE DIVING:

Bronzed streamlined bodies in the tightest fitting wetsuits imaginable descend to the depths of the ocean to see how long they can hold their breath before the light at the end of the tunnel tells them it's time to return to the surface. If you prefer holding your breath and journeying to the outer limits of consciousness to sitting in the bar drinking a beer with your friends, here's how to get started.

1. Watch Luc Besson's dreamily ambient movie, *The Big Blue*, starring Jean Marc Barr as a mystical loon who falls in love with Rosanna Arquette and then dumps her for a dolphin. If that movie doesn't make you hanker for the depths, nothing will.

2. Competitive free diving is currently governed by two world associations: AIDA International and CMAS. There are several disciplines to try out to find which suits you best:

Static apnea: timed breath holding in a swimming pool

Dynamic apnea: underwater swimming in a pool for distance; can be done with or without fins. There are six depth disciplines, which differ in the method of descent

and ascent, of which "no limits" is the most sexy: you
use any means of breath-holding to dive to depth using a
weighted sled and return to the surface along a guideline
with the help of an air-filled bag.

3. Meet other free divers to learn more about the sport,
join an online discussion group, and go to the pool to
practice.

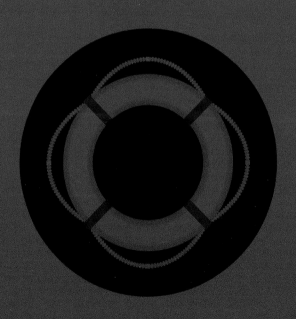

TRAINING

Fortunately, humans have the mammalian diving reflex. That means as soon as you dive to depth you will experience a drop in heart rate; your blood vessels will shrink and fill up with plasma to prevent your lungs from collapsing; and blood is directed away from the limbs to the heart, lungs, and brain.

One training method is the apnea walk. First you spend time spinning your chakras and getting all Zen, then take a few deep breaths, followed by a one-minute breath-hold taken at rest. Then you walk as far as you can without taking a breath (top free divers can walk for over 400 meters). This trains your muscles to operate under anaerobic conditions and to tolerate the buildup of carbon dioxide in the blood stream.

Hyperventilating before a dive lowers the level of carbon dioxide in your lungs and bloodstream, which fools your body into thinking that it is less starved of oxygen than it really is. However, it doesn't raise the amount of oxygen, so most free divers only take three or four oxygenating breaths before a dive.

Always train and dive with a friend. Diving alone is the main cause of serious accidents. If you black out, you need a friend to drag you back to the surface and give you the kiss of life.

100. FLOOD A NEWSGROUP:

There are more ways to skin a cat than to flood a newsgroup, chat room, blog, or bulletin board, but only by a few. From crapflooding to sporgery, here are some imaginative ways to disrupt Internet communities.

TROLLING

A troll is someone who posts insulting or provocative messages to bait other users into responding. Skillful trolls make other users think that they are expressing their true bigoted beliefs (rather than trolling), which generates lots of indignant discussion. Alternatively, trolls pretend to be a seriously misinformed or deluded user (rather than a bigot).

CRAPFLOODING

This is the practice of disrupting discussion websites by flooding them with inane or repetitive postings, to make it difficult for other users to read the genuine posts. It is also a good way of wasting the site's bandwidth and storage space.

It's a lesser form of trolling because it is crude and lacking in subtlety.

SPORGERY

This is the act of sending a flood of posts with fake article headers that make them appear to have been sent by other newsgroup regulars (the word is a composite of *spam* and *forgery*). It's a good way to discredit other users by making it seem like they are sending offensive posts.

HIT-AND-RUN POSTING

This involves writing a long, rambling post that often deviates off topic and takes up a lot of space, then leaving the forum immediately afterwards. This encourages a discussion in which the hit-and-run poster has no intention of participating.

FLAMING

Flamers send deliberately offensive messages, often with no intention to troll (i.e., the flamer isn't trying to fool other posters, just to insult and annoy).

THREAD BREAKING

This refers to the act of sabotaging a forum discussion by posting large chunks of text which makes the thread stretch out until it becomes difficult to follow. Other thread breaking techniques include space breaking, page breaking, and posting long links or large images that take ages to load.

SOCKPUPPETEERING

This is the act of setting up fictional posting accounts to pose as two or more separate users.

BOARD WIPING

On some chat boards, you can wipe the board so that all conversation and posted links disappear. If you do this every ten seconds, it annoys everyone in the chat room and can clear the room very quickly as posters lose interest.

101. GASLIGHTING: MAKE PEOPLE DOUBT THEIR SANITY:

Gaslighting takes its name from the 1944 film *Gaslight* in which the main character is led to believe she is going mad: Charles Boyer fiddles with the gas lamps in the loft which makes the rest of the lamps in the house dim slightly; when Ingrid Bergman notices, Boyer tells her she is imagining things. Hundreds of movies use similar psychological techniques: Harrison Ford makes Michelle Pfeiffer think she's going nuts in *What Lies Beneath*, and Audrey Tautou in *Amélie (The Fabulous Destiny of Amélie Poulain)* plays a strange young woman who gaslights her local grocer. Here are ten ways to destroy your victim's sense of judgment and make them paranoid.

1. Say hurtful things and make them cry, and then, instead of apologizing start recommending treatments for their depression, mood swings, and low self-esteem.

2. Replace their slippers with an identical pair that is two sizes smaller. Do the same thing with their clothes so that they think they have a weight problem, or with their hat to make them think they have swelling of the brain.

3. Replace all the light bulbs in their house with dimmer ones; less light may encourage depression.

4. Move small personal items so that your victim doesn't consciously notice, but subconsciously feels an increasing sense of unease.

5. Remove an item and then return it to a slightly different place when they have wasted an hour searching for it.

6. Each night add a gallon of gas to the gas tank of their car.

7. Mail pornography to their workplace when they are on vacation. It will be opened by someone else in their absence, undermining their reputation.

8. If your victim is a work colleague, chip away at their productivity. For example, if you work in a factory, change a setting on their machine; in an office, steal vital documents before an important meeting or presentation (sabotage a PowerPoint demonstration by adding spelling mistakes).

9. Move furniture around and tell your victim it has always been that way.

10. To develop a habit of compliance in your victim, always enforce trivial demands and make the cost of resistance appear more damaging to self-esteem than capitulation.